The Missing Links

to Making Conservative Principles

and Judeo-Christian Values

the Mainstream of America

The Missing Links
to Making Conservative Principles
and Judeo-Christian Values
the Mainstream of America

And Rescuing Our Country
and Culture from the
Grasps of Liberalism

BASS JOHNSON

THE MISSING LINKS TO MAKING CONSERVATIVE PRINCIPLES AND JUDEO-CHRISTIAN VALUES THE MAINSTREAM OF AMERICA AND RESCUING OUR COUNTRY AND CULTURE FROM THE GRASPS OF LIBERALISM

The views expressed in this work are solely those of the author and do not necessarily reflect the views of the publisher, and the publisher hereby disclaims any responsibility for them.

iUniverse books may be ordered through booksellers or by contacting:

iUniverse
1663 Liberty Drive
Bloomington, IN 47403
www.iuniverse.com
1-800-Authors (1-800-288-4677)

Because of the dynamic nature of the Internet, any web addresses or links contained in this book may have changed since publication and may no longer be valid. The views expressed in this work are solely those of the author and do not necessarily reflect the views of the publisher, and the publisher hereby disclaims any responsibility for them.

Any people depicted in stock imagery provided by Getty Images are models, and such images are being used for illustrative purposes only. Certain stock imagery © Getty Images.

ISBN: 978-1-5320-4737-4 (sc)
ISBN: 978-1-5320-4738-1 (e)

Library of Congress Control Number: 2018904202

Print information available on the last page.

iUniverse rev. date: 04/18/2018

To my husband, Maurice, and our two
wonderful sons, Alex and Jake

Shining Our Light

PRIOR TO THE ELECTION of 2016, millions of Americans knew our beloved country was falling into an abyss and would be pushed over the edge into the dark hole of socialism if the Democratic Party remained in power. After the election, it was reported that Donald Trump had won because he'd heard the voices of Americans no one else had heard. But what was not reported was the reason those in the clique of power had not heard our voices, and that reason is because they did not want to hear us. Our voices were ignored by those in power and in the mainstream media because we went against their agenda. And not only were our voices ignored; our values and beliefs were attacked, misrepresented, twisted, and edited into leftist propaganda. But by the grace of God, we had a few candidates out of a field of many who did hear our voices, and thankfully one of them won. Now all God-loving conservatives have been given more time to save our country and our way of life from the forces that wish to undermine us.

We on the right cannot afford to forget that the election of President Trump is not going to stop the left or the GOP establishment in their efforts to grow a powerful federal government. And neither one of them is going to stop using the current liberal mainstream media and entertainment industry to mobilize the misinformed masses to undermine those of us who believe in limited government, conservative principles, and traditional values. Therefore, it is not the time to rest on our laurels; rather, it is the time to make the light of conservatism and Judeo-Christian values so bright that the masses can't miss what we stand for even if they try. It is time for us to shine in the mainstream and never again allow anyone or anything to dim our light in the spirit of compromise and bipartisanship in order to be more in line with the popular thinking of the day.

CONFRONTING THE MONSTER

PICK ALMOST ANY SPORT that pits teams against each other in a game. Each team puts its players on the field to do battle in order to win the game. Now, what would happen if one team did not have all its positions on the field covered? Well, the opponent would attack that team at those spots and, more often than not, defeat it.

This is what has been happening to God-loving conservatives on a daily basis. Each day, conservatism and Judeo-Christian values lose more and more ground with far too many people because we are either outnumbered or absent in several positions on the field of battle in the very important game for the United States of America. The big battle is between those who want big government to rule over the people (the liberal left and GOP establishment) and conservatives who want to preserve our Constitution in order to keep a limited government controlled by the people, for the people.

Conservative talk radio dominates its position, but it is just one position in the field of battle. It is imperative that we get up to speed in the arena where the mainstream media and entertainment industry currently reigns. This is our biggest, most urgent area at hand that we must address. The left is everywhere! They dominate the internet news feeds, where the big search engines are owned by liberals. The entertainment industry has long been ruled by the liberal left. The movies and television shows that are laced with pro-leftist messages far outnumber anything that represents Judeo-Christian values and conservatism. The fawning over leftist celebrities while shutting out and impugning those who are conservative is commonplace. Even our sports shows are being inundated by the causes of the left. We can no longer afford to dismiss the influence all these things have on a large section of our population. We must develop our own entertainment venues that cater to the masses and the not-so-well-informed people among us. We need to look at each vehicle that the left is using to influence the public and match it.

We do have cable news channels, conservative blogs, and internet news sites doing good work getting the truth out. Like talk radio, these news outlets fill vital positions on the field of battle, and they need to keep doing what they are doing. But also like talk radio, these are venues that cater to the informed among us who want to know the truth about what is going on in the world. Again, our most urgent area is in the mainstream, where the not-so-well-informed people get their news and entertainment. And sadly, many get their news and form their opinions from comedy shows that do political skits and jokes, or dramas that pull at their heartstrings.

I cringe every time I hear someone on our side say that we need Hollywood to make more movies with traditional principles and values, or make comments that maybe Hollywood will wake up and see there is a huge market for more value-based entertainment. No! No! No! We are the ones who need to wake up! Why would we want anyone with a liberal mentality to make any show or report any story that claims to represent Judeo-Christian values and the conservative point of view? Remember the old saying: if you want something done right, you need to do it yourself. Well, we conservatives, we talk radio fans, we who are sick and tired of being mischaracterized, misrepresented, blamed, and persecuted on a daily basis by this huge monster we call the mainstream media and entertainment industry, need to come together to make movies, shows, songs, videos, and internet news feeds that counter this leftist culture that is currently being rammed down our throats. No, we don't need to change Hollywood and the mainstream media to accommodate us. We need to compete with Hollywood and the mainstream media by going head-to-head with them with news and entertainment conservative style.

The left has given us so much ammunition through the years. It will be no problem painting the true picture of liberalism and the true results their policies have had on everything they have touched. But in doing so, it is important not to lose sight of just who we are trying to reach. For the most part, we are dealing with people who pick their candidates because their favorite actor wears that candidate's campaign shirt and believes the liberal way of thinking is what everyone thinks. If we hit them with too much information, we will lose them. So we reach them the same way the left does—with small, repetitive doses mixed in with entertainment and fluff news.

Luckily for us, the left has shown us how it is done. Their blueprint on how to use news and entertainment to influence the general public is out there. We just need to use the same blueprint to counter them with news and entertainment designed for the masses that will show the people that there is another side, that there are other points of view, and that there are millions of people who are in their right minds who disagree with the worldview of the left. Yes, we will have our hits and misses, but so do they. We just need to keep going until the influence the monster has over the public at large is at the very least neutralized. I think we can dominate the mainstream media and entertainment industry in all areas once we get all our positions on the field covered because of one fatal flaw the left has made: they have built their empire on sand. So as long as we build our empire on foundations of rock that are based on what is right instead of what is wrong, truth instead of lies, common sense instead of nonsense, conservatism instead of moderate liberalism, and, last but certainly not least, Judeo-Christian values, we will prevail.

No Stone Left Unturned

THE LIBERAL LEFT'S HUGE advantage is that they have stacked the deck. It is no accident that the vast majority of projects made by Hollywood are created and performed by leftist liberals. It is no accident or fluke of nature that the major search engines and sites on the internet skew left with the news and entertainment they provide. The reason these outlets skew left is that they are owned and operated by the left, who hire leftists to create, write, and perform in their projects. For years the left has been busy using every media tool at their disposal to define and manipulate the culture to their advantage while convincing the general public that everyone agrees with them except for a few lower-than-dirt conservatives and backward-thinking Christians. Once we begin to break into the monopoly the left currently enjoys with the mainstream audience, their hold on the masses will start to crack and crumble.

We need our own networks owned by God-loving conservative groups. What should these network groups do? The same thing the liberal groups do. They must fill the web and airwaves with products designed to entertain, inform, and influence the public, but with conservative leanings and Judeo-Christian values. For example, our channels should be a showcase of conservative-leaning sitcoms, dramas, movies, public service announcements, cartoons, children's shows, soaps, talk shows, political satire shows, songs, videos, and the like. Many of our shows should have lead characters who are likable Christian conservatives who listen to talk radio. Our shows need to have little zingers written into the scripts from time to time to zap the liberals and their agenda (just like they do to us). We must promote on our shows conservative politicians who are fighting the good fight while exposing the Democrats and establishment Republicans for the double-talking, backstabbing, self-serving jackals they are. We need to create shows and movies with plotlines that reveal the true treatment conservatives endure at the hands of liberals. An excellent plotline for a show would be to portray a conservative student threatened with a bad grade by a liberal teacher if the student does not follow the left's view on a particular issue while writing a paper. Another good show plot would be to portray journalists working in a liberal newsroom first seeing a huge story being suppressed to protect the Democrat liberal agenda and then being threatened with the loss of their jobs if they continue to cover the story. Then have talk shows hosted by unapologetic conservatives that will not only invite the stars of those programs on their shows to promote their projects but also follow up with real-life students and journalists who have experienced leftist bullying firsthand at their schools or jobs.

We need to use all the garbage Hollywood and the liberal mainstream media have been pumping out for years and use it against them. Their reporting of and presenting outright lies as facts in news stories in order to push a liberal narrative that have had disastrous consequences for people and their communities. Their blind support of liberal policies and corrupt liberal politicians that have resulted in tragic consequences to the very people and communities they claim to care so much about. I could give many more examples. But if you listen to talk radio, you know what they do, and you know what we need to do. We must get up to speed in the mainstream arena and reach the misguided masses.

We also need radio stations owned by God-loving conservatives that have on-air talent who play music, tell jokes, interview celebrities, and report the news and sports headlines of the day at the top of the hour just like the shows run by the left—but without the liberal bias written into the headlines. These radio outlets are *not* to take the place of conservative talk radio. I can't say enough that conservative talk radio needs to keep doing what it is doing. We need in addition to conservative talk radio, more entertainment shows that will attract and hold the attention of the mainstream crowd. For the most part, these radio programs and stations are nonpolitical. They should be filled with music, sports, celebrity interviews, and on-air antics for the mainstream audience's listening pleasure. These radio shows should, however, poke fun at the left on occasion, support conservative causes, and, most importantly, be ready to go into a full-blown fight mode in conjunction with all our other conservative outlets whenever the left-wing attack machine goes on the warpath against one of our own people, values, or traditions. And our top-of-the-hour news will be news and not a platform used by the left to spew their bias slant of the news onto their unsuspecting audience.

God-loving conservatives need to own search engines and get them in place in order to compete with those run by the left. It should scare the bejesus out of us that all the big search engines are owned by leftists. And it is those search engines that are used by the vast majority of the people when they go on the internet.

We need our own social media and video-sharing websites that are owned and operated by God-loving conservatives. Like everything else, the left own all the main sites. We are already seeing posts and individual users who are favorable to the right and critical of the left being banned from sites owned by leftist groups. This is only going to get worse if we allow the left to monopolize social media. It is important we don't lose a way for conservatives to connect and converse with each other on the internet and get our thoughts and messages out to the masses. This is why it is so important that conservative groups own social networks and video-sharing websites. And we need to promote those sites on our other media outlets and help them grow.

We are indeed living in challenging and exciting times. Technology is changing things so fast that one can only imagine what new outlet will emerge in the future as the latest, greatest way to entertain and inform the public. Whatever emerges, God-loving conservatives must keep up to speed and never again let the left achieve the near monopoly they enjoy today in the area of mainstream news and entertainment. The bottom line is this: if the left is using an outlet to spew their warped vision of the world, then we need to be using the same type of outlet with enough numbers to counter their message and promote our views and our values. We must leave no stone unturned, because we have seen what happens when we do. The snakes multiply under those rocks and come out and bite us.

GETTING STARTED

I REMEMBER BACK WHEN THE federal government was taking the census and they were running a public service announcement using a bus analogy. It went on about how the information they gathered would help the federal government better serve the people and their communities. They explained that the government would use the information gathered in the census to determine, for example, whether or not communities needed additional buses and bus stops. Without this information, they claimed, these communities and the people in them would not know they needed more buses and stops. The PSA ended with the impression that only the federal government can determine and fulfill the needs of the people and their communities. I think the reason that PSA sticks in my mind even to this day is because every time I heard it, I felt insulted. How dare the federal government say that only they can see a need and fill it! How stupid do they think we are? We have the best quality of life in this country not because of government, but because of everyday citizens seeing needs and filling them. Many of our fellow citizens have already fallen prey to the "only government can do it" trap, but I am here to tell you that there are still millions of us in this country who have vision, entrepreneurial spirit, and the intelligence not to rely on the government for our wants and needs. My point in bringing up this remembrance is that there is a great need now in our country that all God-loving conservatives must come together and fill. The government has determined what mainstream media and entertainment they want us to have, and that is our current liberal mainstream. And we right-wingers need to replace their mainstream with one of our own—and we need it ASAP!

Now, I don't know the first thing about how to go out and round up a group of investors in order to form an entertainment network, but I am sure there are those in our conservative talk radio family that do. I don't know the first thing about starting up a cable channel and securing programming for that channel, but I would bet there are those in our conservative talk radio family that do. I would also bet there are many conservative talk radio fans that have pent-up talents that could not find a home for their creative endeavors in Hollywood because they were conservative. And I would bet my bottom dollar that there are those in our conservative talk radio family that have the knowledge and means to start up a conservative-owned search engine for the internet. I am also totally confident that the same can be done for all the other outlets the left currently monopolize and use to their advantage in swaying public opinion.

Notice that I keep referring to the group that needs to bring all these new conservative outlets into fruition as "the talk radio family." This is because, with the exception of some right-wing websites and the Tea Party, which have their roots in talk radio, we talk radio conservatives have been attacked and thrown under the bus by everyone but ourselves and a sliver of politicians in the GOP. In other words, we can trust only ourselves. This is why it is paramount that these endeavors be formed by true conservatives who listen to conservative talk radio and are therefore up to speed on the events of the day and the shenanigans of the left. We cannot afford at this late date to allow the go-along-to-get-along moderate crowd to have any influence on these undertakings as they continue, in the spirit of bipartisanship, to pull us into a country ruled by the leftists and then expect us to still vote for them and smile when they stab us in the back.

The task at hand is a tall order, and one of the most challenging items will be the coming together and assembling of all the people with the talent and know-how in order to make things happen. When the patriots over two hundred years ago knew they had to fight against the British or succumb to their rule, they built up their resistance with like-minded individuals. We need to follow their lead and have fellow conservatives not just at the top executive and creative levels, but at all levels of these endeavors. The patriots also did not march up to King George and tell him what they were doing. We need to do the same and keep our plans in-house until our products are ready to hit the mainstream. In other words, don't go anywhere to talk about these startup channels, stations, internet projects, or whatever, except for known conservative outlets. Now, I don't mean for people to call in to talk radio shows to tell us about a project unless the host invites them to do so, because they have enough on their plates keeping us informed. I mean, for example, they should advertise on conservative websites and talk radio to let us know where we can find their programs so we can tune in; or, if they have job openings, where we can apply. Also, a group setting up a new channel, network, website, or whatever needs to set up shop in a red state (no need to give employment and tax dollars to blue states or pay their union dues). Think of the snowball effect once we get going; not only will we be cutting into the influence of the liberal media, but we will also be creating prominent and behind-the-scenes jobs for our fellow conservatives. Plus it will send a long overdue message to the liberal mainstream media and entertainment industry about their relevance when we can build an audience for projects we created, promoted, and distributed totally on our own and without them.

Now, I don't think anyone on our side will be caught off guard by the full-on assault the left will engage in against our media and entertainment vehicles, but we need to just stay the course and explain that our outlets are nothing more than affirmative action for conservatives. Our endeavors are the first steps toward healing the wounds conservatives have suffered for decades at the hands of liberals in the news and entertainment industries. These outlets will soothe the scars that conservatives bear after years of suffering while being forced to live in the shadows, knowing that if their secret of being a conservative got out they would be ostracized and discriminated against. (Remember: they have shown us how it is done.) Then we follow this up with morning, afternoon, and evening talk shows hosted by conservatives to invite conservative after conservative to come on their shows and tell their stories of the fear and stress they endured while working for and alongside liberal elitists. In addition to those stories, we showcase those who have been targeted by the left to come on these future shows and tell their stories of being crucified for not going along with the groupthink mentality of the so-called champions of tolerance and diversity. I have no doubt that these segments—with citizens telling their stories of having their businesses attacked for following their religious beliefs or being targeted by the IRS because they were a member of a political group the left did not like, and being called racists, haters, and even terrorists by Democrats in the US government and by liberal commentators on the national airways—will trump those who are crying on the liberal shows because of the pain and suffering they endured because of the name of a football team or because someone wished them a merry Christmas.

Once we get all our outlets in place so that we can compete with the left for the hearts and minds of the mainstream crowd, we must work together. We are competing against the left, not each other. We need to support and promote the outlets and projects of our fellow conservatives (providing they are good) in order to chip away at and ultimately topple the liberal influence on the mainstream crowd. This is no time to look at a fellow conservative's project, channel, website, or whatever and go into a competitive mode in an attempt to take it out in order to gain a larger market share. We need each other, and we must stand together and support each other in order to validate our positions in the minds of our targeted audience. Good things will happen, and happen fast, once we expose to the masses that the liberal mainstream is nothing but a slew of hacks from the Democratic Party who have brought nothing but damage to communities, schools, and the very people who vote for them because of their policies.

The task of challenging the mainstream media and entertainment industry is daunting. But once we crack the influence the left has over the mainstream crowd, our efforts will really start to show up at the ballot box, and we can then get more true conservatives in office. We already have the thinking voter's vote, thanks to talk radio, our conservative websites, and a select few in the news media. But it is when the left-leaning, spoon-fed masses come out in droves to vote that we either lose or get too close for comfort. It is these voters we must target and reach using our future mainstream projects. And once we do, the left will forever be rendered to the richly deserved fringe minority status, with them getting less than 40 percent of the vote.

WHAT CAN I DO?

I F YOU HAVE LISTENED to talk radio for any amount of time, you are familiar with the calls from people prior to the election of 2016 that were heartbroken with the direction our beloved country was going. You could hear the frustration in their voices as they described how they felt about seeing the traditions and values that have made this country great being attacked on a daily basis while the very things that were bringing our country down were being promoted and praised. You could also hear the helplessness in their voices and the desire to do something to turn things back around, but they were at a loss as to what that something was. We identify with those callers because we were all feeling the same sense of frustration, helplessness, and desire to do something that would stop this liberal assault on our nation. All God-loving conservatives must remember that feeling and not forget how close we came, prior to the election of President Trump, to losing our country to the likes of Hillary Clinton and the left. But more importantly, we must not rest on our laurels. The election of President Trump has given God-loving conservatives more time to save our country, and we must realize the fight is far from over. And the question is often asked, what more can I do besides calling my representatives? Well, there is something more you can do: be a loyal customer!

All the people who became devastated beyond words when the Democratic Party won the presidency in 2012, just months shy of the Benghazi attack, must never forget that the current liberal mainstream media and entertainment industry helped carry the Democrats to victory. The Democratic Party, which denied requests for extra security for our people in Benghazi, resulting in the deaths of those individuals, won another four years to lead our country. The Democratic Party that lied and blamed a little filmmaker for causing the attack on Benghazi still won the presidency. The Democratic Party that did everything in their power to cover up the details about Benghazi while mocking those who sought the truth still won the presidency. They once again got away with all their lies because the liberal mainstream media and entertainment industry dutifully covered up all their corruption and played cheerleaders for the Democratic Party's agenda. Well, my friends, they got away with it in 2012 but not in 2016, and now is the time to drive the final nail into their coffin. It is time for true God-loving conservatives to compete and defeat the liberal mainstream media and entertainment industry. And all you conservative talk radio listeners—we need your help to accomplish this feat. We need you to be loyal customers!

To all the people who are sick and tired of the Republican Party establishment, which is more concerned with the party than the people and our country, there is something you can do besides complaining to them in an email. Be a loyal customer! If you have a strong desire to rid the Republican party of the RINOs and restore the party to its conservative roots, there is something you can do in addition to lighting up their phone lines. Be a loyal customer! To all the people who lived with nervous fear in the pits of their stomachs during this past election cycle, there is something you can do to keep the GOP and President Trump on course to make America great again. Be a loyal customer!

There is only one thing that will keep our conservative mainstream media and entertainment projects from getting off the ground and ultimately toppling the left's hold over the mainstream crowd, and that is a lack of customers. These entrepreneurs starting up channels, search engines, or any other efforts designed to compete with the left need our support. They can fail only if we fail them. We need to let them know that the same customer base that keeps conservative talk radio in business will keep them in business as long as they thrive to give us good products to support. We need to give these entrepreneurs a built-in audience that will root for their success, give their projects a chance to develop, and then promote their projects to others if and when they hit the mark.

Now, I know everyone can't watch everything, but it is important to watch as much as you can until our conservative mainstream media and entertainment projects get up and running. It would be helpful to have a website that posts the ratings for just our shows so we can see how our shows are doing and determine which new shows need more of us watching in order to give them a chance to survive. Of course, if a show is bad and ultimately needs to go, we must not get discouraged. It happens all the time. We just need to keep going, and we will have success.

My fellow talk radio hosts and fans, we have been through a lot together. It has been mostly frustration and angst during the past several years while we have watched our country slip further and further to the left. But through it all, we have not lost our values and the desire to make our country great again. My friends, we deserve to have a mainstream media and entertainment industry that has our back and celebrates our way of life. And there is no doubt in my mind that once we get rolling, we will not only attract the mainstream crowd but will also snowball into a media outlet bigger than Hollywood. So find your role in building our mainstream media and entertainment industry. Whether it is being a loyal customer, creating a show, writing a song, producing a video, or being part of a team in securing a channel, search engine, social media site, or whatever, we need you to find your role and be a part of the conservative mainstream media and entertainment industry.

PROVEN METHODS

ONCE WE GET ALL our outlets in place, we can start adopting the successful formulas the left uses to influence the masses. One of the most powerful proven methods is the intertwining of mainstream news and entertainment. We must not dismiss or underestimate the influence nonfiction and even fictional television shows and movies can have on the masses. This is especially true when you can intertwine an entertainment piece with real people and events. For example, I know a gentleman who at this writing is in his early seventies. If you talked to him about most issues, you would think he was a conservative. Like us, he is worried and bewildered about the direction the country is going. He believes in a strong work ethic, and he worked his whole life to support his family. As the 2016 elections started to heat up, he asked me what I thought about Hillary Clinton. I told him I would never vote for her because of Benghazi. I reminded him that when our now dead people in Benghazi asked for extra security prior to the attack, she ignored them. Then, during the attack, they asked for help and she sent nothing. Then, to top it all off, she participated in the lies and cover-up in the aftermath. His response to me was that she wanted to do something but couldn't because her hands were tied. He backed up his statement by asking me if I ever watched a television show titled *Madam Secretary* because the show answered all the questions about Hillary and Benghazi. He proceeded to tell me that Hillary had wanted to help but couldn't because her hands were tied by higher-ups. I asked him who the higher-ups were, and he said the show did not say, but the character in the show, who is modeled after Hillary, tried very hard to do something. When I reminded him that it was just a television show, he said he had heard that the show has political connections and they used the show to let the people know what happened. Then he explained that the reason they used the show instead of explaining in the news what really happened in Benghazi was because the Republicans would use all that information to attack the Democratic Party and undo all their good works. I did not ask him what good works he was referring to, because I was afraid he would say "Obamacare," and then my head would have exploded. Anyway, my point is that not all Democrat voters are nonthinkers looking for a handout. This man is not stupid but is a product of the Democratic left-wing propaganda machine. He reads the newspaper, he watches the network morning shows and the network evening news programs, and he glances at the internet network news feeds. So when he watches a television show that fills in the blanks on what is speculated about in his network news sources, he believes it. Even though all that he has seen is a lie and propaganda, his opinion is formed based on the lies because the left-wing machine got the narrative out to all their outlets and he sees what the Democratic Party wants him to see—in not one but several different so-called news sources all saying the same thing. Then various entertainment shows come along and bring what he sees in the news to life in programs filled with drama and emotion that tie all the propaganda up into a nice little package for all to see and understand. It is not true, of course, but it is believed all the same. And that, my friends, is one of the basic formulas the left is implementing in reaching the hearts and minds of the mainstream crowd.

Another powerful tool the left is utilizing to influence the masses is the mainstream talk shows. The mainstream talk shows are a great multitasking tool, which is why there are so many of them. These shows are entertaining and informative, and they provide a wonderful promotional platform for guests to come on and market their projects. These shows also provide a way for the audience to get to know the host and guests on a more personal level because it is presumed that the people on them are being themselves and having an unscripted conversation. And audiences love them, which is why the left has taken them over and made them into progressive propaganda machines. We conservatives are just a small blip in the mainstream talk show circuit compared to the left.

These mainstream talk shows have an influence on the general public in a variety of ways. There is the influence the hosts have on their audience. The left knows that if the hosts can project the image of being caring, in the know, and, above all, cool, some viewers will form an opinion on any given subject based on how the host feels about it. So these shows are filled with leftist hosts that use various methods to ensure their viewers know exactly how the hosts feel about any given subject. One of their favorite tactics to get their views across to their audience is seen in the way they treat certain guests. They gush with praise and admiration over certain guests while asking them fun softball questions, in contrast to glaring at another while asking gotcha questions and rolling their eyes at the answers. Now, to be fair, sometimes liberals are called out on something they have said or done and are asked the hard questions. But that happens rarely. And to be fair, not all conservative guests are set up and attacked. But it does happen frequently. This is especially true if there is a hot issue in the news the left is fanning the flames on while seeking gasoline to pour on the fire. If a right-leaning guest is booked, the host will put him or her on the spot by innocently asking his or her opinion on the matter. This is a salivating moment for the left because they hope to get the conservative celebrity or politician to agree with their view. Or, even better, the guest will say something the left can use to make conservatives look stupid or out of touch. Then, if the liberal host or hostess gets the guest to say something the left can use to advance their leftist agenda, it is fed into the machine, and in the blink of an eye, it is all over the internet news feeds, social media, television, radio, newspapers, and the like. It will pop up on your sports channels during a discussion between the talking heads. Even though the subject has nothing to do with sports, they will find a way to work it in. You will even have people you don't know emailing you about it.

Then there is the influence the mainstream talk shows have over their audiences in the way they present the news. The morning versions have a news reporting segment followed by discussions between the hosts about the news and current events. This is where the liberals use selective reporting by pushing the news they want their viewers to hear while they bury others. It is also where the liberal spin and propaganda are laid on thick. And all these little news and discussion segments are mixed in between a chef coming on to show the proper way to make a salad, celebrity interviews, and segments on the latest fashion trends, so as to not lose the attention of the mainstream crowd.

Then we move into the afternoon, where the left uses emotions to push their agenda along. This is where the viewer often sees the emotional turmoil a guest has endured as a result of an injustice that must be fixed. The afternoon shows are where you will likely hear the stories of the pain and suffering gay couples experience when they are refused service by Christian businesses when planning their same-sex weddings. It is on these shows where the liberal host rarely points out that the refusing shop might not have hate in their hearts but just wants to follow their religious beliefs. And the gay couples are rarely asked by the liberal hosts if they sought out other shops that would cater to their needs. If they were asked, the liberal host would probably find out that the gay couples actively looked for a shop that would have religious objections so they could make a big fuss about it. But no, no, no, suggesting they respect others' religious beliefs and just go someplace else would be offensive to the guest, and anyone who would suggest such a thing is deemed a racist, bigot, or homophobe.

With that we move on to the nighttime talk shows. On the late-night talk shows, humor is mostly used to advance the cause. The jokes are almost always aimed at those who don't march to the beat of the liberal drum. Oh, we get the occasional joke aimed at the left because things are getting so bad that even the liberal host can't ignore it anymore. We on the right get so excited when the liberal host tells a joke that slams the left. We think that finally the liberal host has seen the light, only to be disappointed later on.

I could write several more pages about the things the liberal mainstream talk shows do to propagandize their audience, but that is really not important. What we are going to do about it is the important issue. And what we need to do is use the same successful morning, afternoon, and evening formats that the mainstream crowd currently enjoys, but with God-loving conservatives in charge. And our news segments on our morning shows will tell the audience the truth about the news of the day, while pointing out those in the media who are misleading the public in their reporting of the news. Our talk shows in the afternoon will have segments that will show the emotional turmoil leftist policies have created in the lives of the guests. Then, in the evening, the folly of the left and their stupid voters will no longer go unnoticed in the jokes of the opening monologues and comedy skits. We also need to have conservative-leaning political satire shows in the mix.

Once we have our mainstream talk shows in place, we will have a friendly platform for conservative celebrities and religious leaders to come on and talk about their latest projects, as well as a nonhostile platform for conservative political candidates to promote their campaigns or ideas. We will also have a friendly platform for our conservative talk radio hosts and news bloggers. I think it is important for our conservative talk radio hosts and bloggers to be frequent guests on these shows so the audience can get to know them for the men and women they truly are and not the demonized versions portrayed by the left. But of course, the bread and butter for the mainstream talk shows is the parade of celebrities coming on to promote their latest projects. So you out there in conservative talk radio land with ideas for a script, song, video, or whatever—it's time to get busy because we are on the ground floor and we need your creative endeavors. I already see a vast number of really clever, smart, and funny items posted on conservative online sites all the time that my fellow conservatives have come up with. So I know the talent is out there. We just need talk shows hosted by God-loving conservatives to showcase this talent in mainstream formats that will attract the attention of the masses.

The trickle and the blast are two more very effective tools that the current liberal mainstream media has effectively used to promote their agenda and attack their opposition. The way the trickles are used in the mainstream is why most people don't see the mainstream media as political at all, because the bulk of what is seen and heard is not political or based on an agenda. The masses didn't and still don't see that they have been slowly conditioned to the left's way of thinking by this constant, repetitive, ever-flowing trickle of liberal ideology and propaganda that has been spun into their news and entertainment sources. The trickles are things like a popular character on a show wearing a T-shirt bearing a pro-leftist message, a celebrity wearing a T-shirt promoting a Democratic candidate, a one-line zinger aimed at the right on a sitcom, a plotline in a drama series that raises awareness on a liberal cause, a talk show segment where the liberal slams Christians and conservatives, talking heads on the sports channels wringing their hands about how we must be more tolerant to some leftist movement, and on and on. These ever-flowing little trickles that seep into the hearts and minds of the mainstream crowd and influence their way of thinking are what we need to counter in our mainstream with reinforcing trickles of our own.

Then there is the dreaded blast. That is when a story, statement, event, or whatever suddenly explodes all over the media in the blink of an eye. The left owns the blast because they own the bulk of the current media outlets. It is also another very important reason why we must have more than one of all the different types of outlets. If we have only one channel, for example, our blasts to counter their blasts will be a whimper, and our trickles will be a drop in the bucket. There is truly strength in numbers, and the more different types of outlets and variety of products we have on those outlets, the more effective our conservative blasts and trickles will be.

Thankfully, it is a great time to be starting up our conservative mainstream media and entertainment industry while the old liberal guard is scrambling to keep up with technology and adjust to an ever-changing market place. Also, thanks to the internet, everyday people can post things they have created and have a chance for them to be seen by millions of people. Many of our fellow conservatives have taken advantage of this and given us an abundance of excellent material that can get our outlets off the ground and keep us going while new products are being produced.

And finally, as we are learning from the left how to use these proven methods in order to reach the hearts and minds of the mainstream masses, the left is also showing us what not to do. The left has ruined award shows for the average viewer, and since the election of President Donald Trump, they are in the process of turning off even more viewers to the rest of their entertainment because of their constant venom against those who disagree with their agenda. We must guard against making these same mistakes by not by getting too overbearing, too in-depth, or too preachy when making our points in the mainstream arena.

MEAT AND POTATOES
ALONG WITH SOME SIDES

I N OUR NEVER-ENDING FLOW of conservative principles and Judeo-Christian values, along with examples of liberal failures that are going to be mixed into our mainstream entertainment, we will have our meat-and-potato issues along with our side issues. The meat-and-potatoes issue for the Democratic Party is to create a powerful federal government that they control while convincing the general public they are working to make everything fair and equal for everyone. Their solution to every problem is more federal government oversight and control. Their sideshow distractions are designed to project the image that they are the party that cares and to keep their opposition in a constant state of turmoil and wear us down while they take over the country. Their sides are things like the bathroom issues, Confederate symbols, the war on women, the names of sports teams, the war on Christmas, race wars and anything else they can think of.

Our meat-and-potato issues will be limited government, states' rights, the preservation of our Constitution, and our keeping the power and freedom with "we the people." And our side issues will be the vast number of irreconcilable differences we have with liberal Democrats. Our sides issues will meet their side issues head-on, debunk them, and turn the tables on the left so the liberals will be the ones put on the defensive. Every one of their side issues can be turned around and debunked. None of their arguments hold up when they run into challenges, truth, and logic, which is why they do everything in their power to shut us down so we are not heard. Talk radio and our conservative media do a good job exposing all the nonsense of the left so it is obvious what the liberals are doing and why. We just need to convert what we know about liberals, along with our ideas, and weave it into mainstream media formats and begin presenting it to the masses.

Now, our goal should not be to defeat the left in a way that will leave the left-leaning masses to bemoan what could have been if only the Democrats could be in charge. Our path to victory and freedom from the left and to restore America as it was founded is to allow the leftists to defeat themselves while not taking us down with them. States' rights are our golden ticket to victory. With states' rights, the states will once again compete with each other. Red states and counties that run with conservative principles will reap what they sow. Blue states and counties with liberal and moderate policies will reap what they sow. Thanks to the elites in our federal government and our current liberal mainstream media, the left has reversed this concept, and the results have been disastrous for everyone but the upper-class establishment. The liberal left has made an absolute mess of almost everything they touch, and they have reaped undeserved rewards for their inner circles while making the rest of us pay the price.

We must waste no time in telling our mainstream audience that we believe things run much smoother and that more opportunities are created in areas run with conservative principles and Judeo-Christian values. We will make it abundantly clear to our mainstream audience that the liberal policies of the Democratic Party bring us down and we want to shield our communities from the ill effects of those policies. We must inform the masses that there are millions of us that are offended by what the liberal Democrats have done over the years and then remind the mainstream crowd of all the times the left pushes for change in ways, traditions, or whatever, even if just one person is offended. We will make it clear that we do not want to break up the union and we are not the ones using the federal government to force this country into a one-size-fits-all common ground box. We will let the mainstream crowd know that we wish well those states and counties that want to continue on the path of Democratic Party rule but we vehemently oppose being dragged under their jurisdiction against our will and having our tax dollars taken from us to pay for things that millions of us don't want or believe in.

Now we must not look at the mainstream crowd that leans left in the same way as we do the militant left. Some are like children that have been spoiled and coddled and think the world is here to take care of their needs because that is what the Democrats are telling them. Others have been convinced they are victims and encouraged by the left to be disruptive when things don't go their way. Then the rest of the left-leaning masses have been bought with government perks or promises pushed by Democrats and by Republicans in name only, commonly called RINOs. Either way, we must break away from them using states' rights and individual freedom so they can make their own choices and live with those choices without bringing the rest of us down with them in the process. I predict that most will find that the grass is not greener on the liberal side and will make their way back home to our side once we have a mainstream media and entertainment industry that works in conjunction with talk radio and conservative news to reject all the blame the Democrats hurl our way and does not cover up all the failures of liberalism.

As for those leftist ideologues and elite establishment types, they must finally reap what they have sown. Our mainstream media will shine the light of hypocrisy on all the wealthy political establishment—the upper-class businesspeople, Hollywood celebrities, fashion designers, and socialite elites that support the Democratic Party— forcing them to finally put their money where their mouth is and start paying for all they have promised to their rank-and-file voters out of their own fat-with-cash pockets. The mainstream crowd has already been conditioned to hate the rich and already has the mind-set that the rich should pay for everything, so it is going to be very rewarding to see the mainstream crowd turn on these elites once we start forcing the issue in the mainstream arena. Now, I am not talking about all rich people—just the liberal ones and the compromising RINOs. But don't hold your breath that they will fork over their millions and billions, but it is going to be fun watching them squirm and backtrack once the bright light of hypocrisy is shining down on their heads in the mainstream of America. And the liberal and RINO elite will have nowhere to run and hide once our conservative mainstream drowns out their liberal mainstream! It is going to be a beautiful thing and a long overdue treat for our side.

In getting started, we will inform the masses that there are millions of people in this country that strongly disagree with the direction the left wants to take the country in, and that we want states' rights to preserve our way of life. We will promote that it is okay to be different, and that it is okay to have different wants, views, needs, and desires. We want to be free to be different, and it is not right to have the rich and powerful using the federal government and our judicial system to force us into a one-size-fits-all society while they pat themselves on the back for crossing over the aisle.

Public service announcements (PSAs) are a great way to get our messages out in front of the mainstream. I have twenty-six public service announcements ready to go. And when they run in the mainstream arena in conjunction with our reinforcing trickles laced into our entertainment, it will make a huge impact on the mainstream crowd. One PSA should run for about two weeks, and then the next one, and so on. And remember: these are not designed to reach the militant left; they are to reach those in the mainstream that have been influenced by the left. And notice the steady drumbeat in almost all of them that reinforces our meat-and-potato issues of states' rights, preserving the Constitution, and keeping power with the people. It is repetitious but necessary.

PUBLIC SERVICE ANNOUNCEMENTS

Why Can't We All Just Get Along?

W HY CAN'T WE ALL just get along? This very question has been asked by many over the years. Well, I am here to help those who have pondered this question understand one of the main reasons why harmony has eluded us. It is because, just as in today's times, all throughout history there have been constant battles between forces that want to control others and those that don't want to be controlled. The forces that want to control others have willing allies of people eager to give up their freedom and independence in order for a controlling body, such as government, to provide for them. Then there are the people who are freedom-loving souls that don't want or need a bunch of control freaks, particularly those in government, interfering in their lives. They want instead a smaller, less intrusive government that does not infringe on their God-given rights and individual freedoms.

We would go a long way toward getting along with each other if we would recognize that people are different. We have different desires, wants, needs, values, and beliefs. And that is okay. We don't have to be, and should not be, forced to live in a one-size-fits-all society. But that is not what the control freaks of the world want, and they never stop in their efforts to gain control over the people, money, and resources.

The control freaks are those who want to force their views and rules onto the people in order to control your way of life while taking whatever they want from whomever they want for whatever reasons because they believe they are the smart ones and they know what is best for the common good. The political establishments in both the Democratic Party and GOP work hand in hand in the spirit of bipartisanship and compromise to force the people in this country under the jurisdiction of a powerful one-size-fits-all federal government that they control because they think they know what is best for everybody.

The 2016 election saw the political establishment control freaks in both parties suffer defeat at the ballot box. In the aftermath, we saw the political establishment on the GOP side wiping egg off their faces and the Democratic Party weeping and lashing out in anger. Well, we conservatives want everyone who wants to continue to vote for government control and to live under their rule to be free to do so. We conservatives want to get along, and we hope others want to get along with us when we want to go back to a smaller, less intrusive government. We conservatives vehemently oppose sending the bulk of our hard-earned dollars to a big, squandering federal government and then ask them to do things for us. We want to keep the bulk of our hard-earned dollars so we can take care of ourselves and our families as we see fit. We want to make our own decisions, support our own causes, chart our own courses, and worship as we please. In other words, we conservatives want to be free.

Shifting the bulk of the power away from the federal

government and back to the states is the way for all sides to get more of what they want. We have fifty states, and each state is divided up into counties. We all don't have to do the same things and use our money and resources in the same ways. Those who want to live under less government control can do so in conservative-run states and counties. Those who want government heavily involved in their day-to-day lives can continue to elect Democrats and their establishment friends. And as for the control freaks in the Democratic Party and GOP establishment, they will still get to control people; their power will just be limited in conservative areas that adhere to the Constitution and freedom for the people. It is a win-win and a huge step in all of us getting along with each other. Thank you for listening, and God bless America!

***************************PSA***************************

Why Are There So Many Rich Democrats?

Why are there so many rich Democrats? Are they not the ones that support political candidates that claim to be fighting for the poor and middle class? Are they not the ones denouncing the rich for not paying enough in taxes so it can be redistributed back into the village in order for things to be more equal and fair? Why are so many liberal Hollywood stars, East Coast celebrities, and high-society types that support the Democratic Party still extremely wealthy, still living in mansions, driving fancy cars, wearing pricey designer clothes, and traveling to the destinations of their choice for first-class getaways? Why do they spend millions every year planning big, fancy fundraising parties and events so they can invite their rich liberal Democrat friends over so they will give large chunks of money to a Democrat candidate who will then go out and give speeches on how he or she is going to make things more fair for everyone by making the rich pay more? What a farce!

If these people truly meant what they were saying and wanted everything to be fair and equal, these upper-class liberal Democrats would significantly downsize their lifestyles and give the money that they save back to the poor. They also would not spend loads of dough on fancy fundraising parties. Instead they would skip the party and give that money directly to those who are less fortunate than they are. And if you think their deep pockets stop at the East Coast and West Coast high-society celebrity types, think again. Their money is dwarfed compared to what the Democrats in the big business world have at their disposal. They have billions. And have you ever wondered how Democrat politicians become rich themselves while serving in politics, while the lower and middle classes that vote for them remain stuck with little chance to better their lot in life? Why does so much of the money and resources stay in the hands of these rich progressive Democrats instead of going to help those who are less fortunate? The answer is simple. They are all hypocrites, and their phony compassion for the poor and middle class is just like a fictional Hollywood movie filled with imagery and sound but no reality.

We conservatives think it is high time for these rich Democrats to start putting their money where their mouth is and start paying for all the things they promise their voters instead of putting the burden on the working-class taxpayer and running up a huge national debt that is going to burden us all for generations. These rich elite Democrats and their supporters need to start paying for all their promises out of their own bloated pockets. Now, I realize that over time you Democrats, along with your rich supporters, will probably go broke, but you can either work harder to make more money or stop making promises that you expect others to pay for. So either pay up or shut up because the American people are tired of getting the shaft and seeing our opportunities shrink along with our paychecks because of Democratic Party policies.

The 2016 election cycle highlighted the fact that we are at a crossroads in this country, and the ever-growing, bloated, out-of-control federal government was the reason. We hope and pray President Trump will continue to hear the voices of the people who make this country work, so we the people can say goodbye to the crushing regulations, fees, and taxes levied on the people by the feds under Democrat rule that were drying up our opportunities to achieve our American dreams. Thank you for listening, and God bless America!

***************************PSA***************************

The Blame Game

So many people have gotten caught up in the blame game of the Democratic Party. Oh, these Democrat politicians and their allies in the media love to blame Christians, conservatives, men, Republicans, white people, talk radio, and the bogeyman for all the injustices of the world. Well I, for one, on behalf of the millions of Americans who get blamed for all the ills of the world, would like to set the record straight. The Democratic Party and their lineages are not the innocent crusader of social justice that they would like you to believe. Did you know it was the Democratic Party that fought to maintain slavery against the Republicans, who were led by Abraham Lincoln? Did you know it was Democrats who ordered the fire hoses turned on the civil rights protesters in Birmingham back in the sixties? It was also a Democrat governor that stood in the doorway of a state university to block black students from attending the school. Did you know that a late United States Senator in the Democratic Party who was praised and respected by his fellow Democrats, including the Clintons, was a recruiter for the Klan? Did you know it was government led by the Democratic Party that passed the "Indian Removal Act" that moved the Indians off their land? And don't get me started on how they attack and try to destroy any woman or Hispanic person who disagrees with their views or threatens their power.

The Democratic Party needs to be reminded that those who live in glass houses should not throw stones. And those who vote for the Democrats year after year need to know the true character of the party they are voting for and putting in power. Now, our intent is not to redirect anger toward the Democrats for their many past crimes and injustices. Our intent is to educate the people so they will not fall prey to the rhetoric of the Democratic Party and have their hearts filled with anger, resentment, hate, and fear. Those emotions can get out of control and destroy lives and property, as we have unfortunately seen all too often in the news. Conservatives want to educate the people as to the real reason why so many oppose the Democratic Party and why the Democrats falsely accuse everyone who disagrees with them of being racist, xenophobic, misogynistic, or whatever else they can think to accuse us of. The reason for all the slander, fear tactics, and mudslinging that goes on in politics is that the Democratic Party wants to grow and control the powers of the federal government so they can rule over us. And they will say and do anything to get elected in order to do just that. Conservatives want to block the efforts of the Democrats and limit the power of the government, keep the power with the people, and preserve the Constitution. That is the big divide and the reason Democrat politicians and their friends in the media replace truth and reality with outrageous political rhetoric and false accusations.

Conservatives want everyone to know that we want what is best for everyone, as we always have. And we believe that what is best for everyone is to have a limited government that puts an emphasis on personal freedom for the people instead of an emphasis on control of the people. It is our desire for less government that brings out the wrath of the Democratic Party and causes them to slander conservatives with every ounce of their being. We hope that, with the election of President Trump, our nation can come together by going back to states' rights and a limited federal government. Then those areas still wishing to live under the rule of the Democrats and their ideas can pool their money and resources together in their state or county and do so. And the freedom-loving souls that want to be protected from the control policies of the Democratic Party can live under the laws of liberty, freedom, and our Constitution.

This concept is not new, by the way. It was more or less

how this nation ran before Democrat politicians started using the federal government and our courts to force us all under their government rule and use the media talking heads to attack all those who dared to disagree with their policies by labelling them racists, sexists, bigots, xenophobes, misogynists, and a host of other unflattering terms. But today is a new day, and hopefully we will continue to reject those forces that wish to define us and control us, so we can finally come together in the spirit of liberty and freedom. Thank you for listening, and God bless America!

***************************PSA***************************

Border Security and Immigrants

One of the many lies told by the Democratic Party is that Americans who are fighting to secure the borders hate immigrants and want to bust up families. Well, nothing can be further from the truth. Those who want strong borders want what is the best for everybody, and we know without a shadow of a doubt that the worst thing for the vast majority of the people regardless of race or where they came from is for the Democratic Party and their cronies to gain control over this country and set policies. The Democratic Party and their rich supporters, along with the establishment types in the Republican Party, called RINOs, are the ones that work to make sure the rich get richer while the rest of us stay stuck in our place. Yes, you heard that right. The Democratic Party, their wealthy donors, and RINOs have made an unholy alliance in order to reach their ultimate goal. And that ultimate goal of these upper-class establishment types is to ensure that their kind, the elitists, will forever remain in power, their wealth protected, and that the money will continue to flow their way while they keep the rest of us stuck in our place.

These ruling-class elites in the Democratic Party and GOP kept our borders wide open and actively encouraged immigrants to come to America. They saw all these immigrants flooding in as their future voters and their tickets to continued power and control over our country and its people. These Democrats and RINO elites attempted to secure the votes of the immigrants with promises of government benefits to forever tip the scales in their favor come election time and to transform our country from a freedom-loving, power-to-the-people type of government to a government run by them, the ruling upper class. Thankfully the election of Donald Trump has set back their plan, but they are not giving up, and everyone needs to know what is truly going on with immigration.

The Democratic Party and their cheerleaders in the media, along with the RINOs in the GOP, have pushed the narrative that we need immigrants to do the jobs Americans won't do. That argument was never true, because Americans did do those jobs, but certain businesses found that they could get the immigrants to do the same jobs for much lower pay. So those businesses lobbied government politicians to let immigrants cross into our country and take the jobs. So as the immigrants flooded into our country, more and more Americans lost their jobs, and more and more immigrants were taken advantage of and used to work long hours for little pay. It is a winning situation for the political elites because they continue to get the votes and donations from the businesses that want the cheap labor while securing the future votes of the immigrants by giving them government benefits and promising them even more government perks once they get reelected. Of course, these government benefits and handouts come at the expense of the working-class taxpayer and an ever-increasing national debt. Oh, they say they will make the rich pay, but these political establishment types *are* the rich, and they never make themselves pay. What did happen is that our national debt ballooned out of control. Working-class Americans who were lucky enough to keep their jobs saw their take-home pay shrink as more and more was taken out of their earnings to pay for the costs of others. And as immigrants were moved into the areas where the poor and middle class lived, those areas struggled to accommodate the influx of immigrants. Their resources and schools were challenged like never before, while the areas of the rich and powerful were shielded from the negative effects of open borders.

Thankfully the election of President Trump means America can finally secure its borders. But conservatives believe that the supporters of open borders should pay for the needs of the illegal immigrants until it can be determined by vetting who needs to go and who should be put on the path to citizenship as self-supporting, assimilated citizens. It can be called the "support until we deport" plan. It is the perfect plan because never before has the bulk of the wealth in this country been on one side—the side pushing for open borders. So all the millionaires and billionaires that supported the Democratic Party and political establishment's push for open borders need to house all the illegal immigrants in their posh areas and support them—not with tax dollars but with money out of their own pockets, because they caused a big mess in this country and made us all less safe. And they did it not out of compassion for the immigrants, as they have claimed, but to use the immigrants to gain political power and pad their own greedy pockets. Thank you for listening, and God bless America.

***************************PSA***************************

Why America Is Different

Why is America different? Some say America was never any different from the rest of the world, and those people could not be more wrong. America is different. It is the first country since its founding that was not run by upper-class rulers that controlled the people. Instead it shifted the power away from a ruling class by limiting the power of government. It allowed the people to have the power and control over their own lives. And it was this very thing that gave birth to the American dream that allowed ordinary people the freedom to dream their dreams and the opportunities to achieve those dreams. It was not that Americans were better than people from other nations; we were just free to become better and improve our lot in life. And many of us did!

Today's independent-minded Americans, the same type of Americans that made this country great, have witnessed their personal freedoms and opportunities evaporate little by little with every common ground compromise the rich and powerful that run our federal government make with themselves. This shift in power that flows away from the people and gives it to the federal government is what we conservative Americans are fighting against. We want to limit the power these federal government politicians and their fat cat donors have over our lives and shift it back to the people and the states they live in. This is what we mean when we say we want to take our country back. We want to return to the days of a government by the people for the people, instead of a powerful federal government that controls the people.

Hopefully the election of President Donald Trump will be a huge step in foiling the plans of the Democratic Party elite and the tagalongs in the GOP because under their leadership our federal government has become no different from what our founding fathers fought against—a government set up such that the ruling class controls the people, the money, and the resources; the rich continue to get richer and the poor get poorer; and an ever shrinking middle class goes down instead of up. And if you think the federal government run by the Democrats is your crusader that is going to get even with the rich for you, think again. You people need to open your eyes and look at reality. The Democratic Party and their big-money donors, along with the establishment types, are the richest of the rich, and their control over the federal government is one of the very reasons they got richer while the rest of us bounced around in a second- or third-class existence. Oh, they talk a good game about fairness and equality, but that is all it is—*talk*.

Now, for those of you that want to continue to keep your faith in the Democratic Party and are okay with the plans these rich big-government types have for you, then fine. Go for it, but don't force that lifestyle on those of us who want more out of life and the opportunity to pass on an even better life to our children. If living off of government benefits and programs the ruling elite throw your way is how you want to live your life and that is the lifestyle you want to pass down to your kids, we think that is sad, but we honor your right to make those choices for you and your family. We conservatives just don't want that lifestyle forced on the rest of us that wish to live a life beyond the safety nets and big-government control. We want to limit the power of the feds and preserve the Constitution and our freedoms. Then we can be free from the shackles of an overbearing federal government and free to reach for the brass rings and achieve our American dreams. Thank you for listening, and God bless us all.

**************************PSA**************************

Democrats against the Independence of Women

The Democratic Party, the liberal media, and progressive educators are constantly lamenting that Republicans, conservatives, and most men are against the advancement of women. You hear the liberal Democrats say things like "Conservative men won't vote for a particular candidate because she is a woman." It does not seem to matter that conservative Republican men have supported and voted for many women that have run for public office in this country. It happens all the time. But you don't hear the liberal Democrats talking about that. They are too busy male-bashing and telling women how they don't need a man, but they are quick to convince women that they do need government to fight for their advancement in the world. These liberal educators, politicians, and media types are implying that the average woman is not as capable as a man to go out into the world and earn a top salary, get hired, get elected, own a business, or support her own lifestyle without the government run by the Democratic Party by her side to fight for her, pay for her health care needs, and open doors for her in the workplace and political arena.

These progressive liberals cheer when the Democrats hold up women activists as role models who demand others' pay for their lifestyle choices while ignoring or diminishing the accomplishments of conservative women, because they dared to get ahead without the government holding their hand. Take Margret Thatcher, for instance. What a great role model for little girls and women not just in America but around the world as well. Margret Thatcher held the highest office in her country as the prime minister of the United Kingdom. The fact that Margret Thatcher was a woman did not hold her back and prevent her from reaching great heights on the world stage. But all throughout Mrs. Thatcher's career, she was viciously attacked and undermined by leftist liberals in the Democratic Party, the so-called champions of women. In fact, even when Mrs. Thatcher passed away, the Democrats in the US Senate blocked a resolution to honor this great lady. What was Margaret Thatcher's crime, in the eyes of these progressive liberals in the Democratic Party, that warranted so much of their hatred and scorn? She was a conservative who believed in a limited government. The Democratic Party hates this. They want a big government that they preside over that controls the money, the resources, the businesses, the health care, the people, and everything else.

So whenever you hear a left-wing Democrat say that the people on the right will not vote for a particular candidate because she is a woman, you now know that is a big fat lie. It is not one's gender—or race, for that matter—that prevents a right-winger from supporting a political candidate; it is one's ideology! And the ideology of the left that wants to force their policies of control down the throats of the American people will not get the vote of those of us who want a limited government, individual freedom, and the preservation of the Constitution. But hey, if all the Democrats want is for a woman to be president, let us all unite behind a conservative woman who is strong on preserving the Constitution and limiting the power of the feds. We don't need a RINO who just says she is a conservative; we need a true conservative in the likes of the late, great Margret Thatcher. Then, together, we can break that glass ceiling. Thank you for listening, and God bless America!

**************************PSA*************************

The Secretary

One of the favorite lines of the Democratic Party is that it is unfair for a rich man to be in a lower tax bracket than his secretary. Then they parade around a bunch of rich liberals who agree that it is unfair that they are in a lower tax bracket than their secretaries and vow to support the Democrat candidate so they can correct this injustice. This is a farce, of course, and is designed to fool the people into voting for Democrats. Because if those stories were investigated, we would no doubt find that wealthy people in lower tax brackets than their secretaries used the layers of bureaucracy in our tax codes to legally finagle themselves into that lower bracket. Also, it is important to note that if rich liberals want to pay more in taxes, they can regardless of their tax bracket. Nothing is preventing any rich liberal Democrat from paying more; they just choose not to. So instead of paying more in taxes, they create the illusion of wanting to pay more by lamenting the fact that some rich people are in a lower tax bracket than their workers.

The layers and layers of bureaucracy in the tax codes created by politicians are the best friends of the wealthy and political elite. It is in these layers of bureaucracy that the Democrat politicians and establishment RINOs can use the tax code to benefit themselves and their rich cronies. It is also where they go after those that threaten their power. But they don't want the average voter to focus on all the layers of bureaucracy written into our tax code. They want the voters to focus on the poor secretary and her tax bracket.

Conservatives believe we should go to a simple tax code that strips away this bureaucratic playground of the elite upper class. We believe a simple flat tax without all the bureaucracy will force everyone to pay their fair share and keep more money in the hands of the people who earn it, including secretaries! But regardless of what happens to our tax code in the future, the American people need to remember that anyone can always pay more in taxes or donate more to causes.

So the next time you hear a rich liberal agree with the Democrats that they should pay more in taxes, be sure to remind them that nothing is stopping them from paying more now. They can do it today if they want to, but they usually don't. They are too busy finding ways they can pay less in taxes, like the rest of us. So don't fall for their political ruses about secretaries and tax brackets. Instead, get even with the rich that dodge paying their fair share; support a simple flat tax code without all the political bureaucracy. Thank you for listening, and God bless America!

**************************PSA***************************

Minimum Wage

Some politicians want to force businesses to pay an ever-increasing minimum wage for starter jobs instead of encouraging people to use these entry-level positions to gain work experience and then use that work experience as a stepping stone to a better job with more responsibilities and more pay. Most people know that workers are not supposed to stay stagnant in low-skilled starter job positions. People are supposed to learn and grow so they can advance and earn more pay. This helps the employer by being able to delegate more responsibility to their workers in exchange for more pay, and it helps the workers because they gain more pay and more experience when they take on more responsibilities.

Starter jobs have always been a great way for young adults just starting out or others who are unskilled in the labor force to get an opportunity to earn some cash and gain work experience so they can advance in the workforce and earn more pay. And that is how it is designed to work. But an ever-increasing minimum wage forced on businesses by government that is designed to enable workers to stay stagnant in starter jobs and not grow into taking more responsibility in order to earn that extra pay hurts the employer and dries up opportunities for those just starting out in the workforce. As more and more entry-level starter jobs are being kept by those who won't advance in the workforce in order to earn more pay, but instead are demanding government force businesses to pay them a higher minimum wage so they can raise their families on wages earned in these entry-level starter positions, more and more job openings are drying up for those just starting out, and more business are finding themselves struggling to make ends meet. Small businesses were the hardest hit in those areas that raised the minimum wage, and sadly, many had to close their doors because they could not afford to pay the higher wages for these entry-level starter jobs.

Conservatives believe the government should not force an ever-increasing minimum wage on businesses. Not supporting an ever-increasing minimum wage so people can support a family on these low-skilled entry-level starter positions is not mean or oppressive; it is good for business and good for the workers. It is good for the workers because it gives employees the incentive to learn and grow in their work experience so they can move up from the starter job to make more money and gain even more experience in order to advance even further. And whenever a worker moves up, it creates a job opening for the next person just starting out to take that entry-level position. And it is good for the businesses because they increase their chances of staying in business when they are not forced to pay a living wage for these low-skilled entry-level starter positions.

So now you know why conservatives disagree with Democrats when it comes to the minimum wage. But we conservatives believe in freedom. So if all business owners that support the Democratic Party want to double or even triple what they pay their workers for these starter job positions, we conservatives think they should be free to do so. Thank you for listening, and God bless America!

**************************PSA**************************

Make the Left Pay

Listen up! For all you people out there that have bought into the rhetoric of the Democratic Party and their promises to get even with the rich and make them pay for their greedy ways, you need to open your eyes and see the staggering wealth that the Democratic Party, their political leaders, and their rich supporters have. Many are celebrities, athletes, media personalities, and business tycoons that are multimillionaires, and some are even billionaires. These rich Democrat supporters call on others to support the extremely wealthy Democratic Party so they can get even with the rich and make things fair and equal for everybody. What a farce! These people are no different from the rich people they claim to despise for not paying their fair share. Oh, some give to charities and support causes, but so do the other wealthy individuals that get chastised by the Democrats. The only difference is that the mega-wealthy who support the Democratic Party are given a pass. Their wealth is not targeted, and their achievements are praised by leftist politicians and the liberal media. The rich that do not support the efforts of the Democrats to grow and control government are targeted, attacked, and labeled as greedy.

The Democrats and their liberal supporters also love to condemn the Republicans for being a good-ole-boy club that gives promotions, jobs, and perks to their friends and family while bypassing others who are more worthy. And again, the liberal Democrats and their supporters do the very same thing and are no different from those they criticize. In fact, they are a notorious insiders' club packed with their cronies. But again, the Democrats give those who support their party a complete pass.

Conservatives think it is long overdue for these wealthy Democrat politicians and their supporters to start putting their money where their mouth is. The Democrat politicians have been saying for years that they want things to be more fair and equal. In the past, those Democrats called for those making over $250,000 a year to pay much more in taxes. So why don't all the Democrat millionaires and billionaires liquidate all their assets and adjust their lifestyles so they can live on a $250,000-a-year budget and give all the rest away to those who are less fortunate? Just think of the staggering amount of money that would be! It would be billions of dollars that would be pouring in every year because these people make a lot of money. Nothing is stopping any of these progressive liberal hypocrites from doing just that. They could do it at any time, but they don't, and they won't, because it is all a show and all a ruse to get people to vote for Democrats so the elite can grow the power of the government and ensure the money and power stay with those in the clique. And as for the rest of the people who vote for the Democrats with the hope that things will be more fair and equal, they are once again left on the outside looking in.

Conservatives believe that people would be far better off if they learned to depend on themselves instead of being fooled by slick politicians into depending on government for their wants and needs. That is why we conservatives want a smaller, less intrusive federal government, restore states' rights, and keep the power with the people. That way the bulk of our money and power stays with the people and away from the elite establishment types in the Democratic Party and GOP.

But for those who want to continue to vote for the Democrats because of some benefit, perk, or promise they gave to you, we conservatives believe you should have that right. Just don't force the rest of us to pay for it and live under their jurisdiction. Instead, make all the millionaires and billionaires who support the Democratic Party use their money to fulfill all the perks and promises they have made to their voters. And again, nothing is stopping the millionaires and billionaires who support the Democratic Party from adjusting their lifestyles and giving the bulk of their money away to the less fortunate Democrat supporters so things in the village will be more fair and equal. They could do it today, and nobody—not even Donald Trump— would stop them. Thank you for listening, and God bless America!

*************************PSA**************************

Freedom Unities Us; Forced Unity Divides Us

The Democratic Party and RINO Republicans love to say that we are stronger together, so we must compromise and find common ground on all the issues facing the nation. All this sounds good, but in reality the only people getting stronger are the politicians, their rich donors, and their friends in the media that help sell this phony narrative to the general public. Well, thankfully, more Americans are waking up to the fact that the more we allow the power-hungry political establishments to force us to compromise on our way of life in order to find common ground so we can supposedly be united as one with the world has only benefitted the upper-class elites and their cronies. And yes, I said "the world," because the establishment elitists in our federal government not only want to control the people of this nation; they also want to take their power around the world so they can align themselves with the elites of other nations in order to form a global establishment that rules over all the people on earth. Because it is not enough for the Democrat politicians, RINOs, and their upper-class supporters to just suck up all the money and power away from the people in this country; their greed wants it all.

Prior to the 2016 election, it was increasingly obvious to anyone with a brain or the guts to open his or her eyes and honestly see reality that the Democratic Party, their cheerleaders in the media, and GOP RINOs had corrupted our federal government for their own benefits in order to enrich themselves with money and power. Their false compassion for the people in this nation has been obvious to conservatives for decades. Hopefully, with the election of President Trump, the establishment elite in both political parties will be blocked from inflicting their self-serving poison on the people and we can go back to states' rights, power to the people, and the preservation of our Constitution.

Conservatives believe that we are not stronger together when we are forced to compromise away our principles, values, and ways of life in order to have one-size-fits-all solutions to problems and issues. We spend so much time, so much effort, and so many resources fighting each other. We need to stop fighting each other, come together, and rejoice in our differences. We need to stop trying to conquer each other and forcing our fellow citizens to live the way we want them to live. It is time to come together and let our differences shine with states' rights. With states' rights, we can have liberal areas, conservative areas, and moderate areas. And neither side should be forced to support things they do not believe in or forced to conform to the principles and values set by Washington politicians. I hope this last decade has taught us all that being forced together by politicians so we can fit into their common ground box never makes us stronger and certainly does not unite us. It only generates animosity between us. Thank you for listening, and God bless America!

****************************PSA***************************

Independence vs. Dependency

The Democratic Party, when it comes to the groups they supposedly want to help, are like those parents you hear about on the news that make their own child sick so they can get favorable attention, donations, and credit for taking care of their sick kid. Then there are the rank-and-file Democrat voters who have been conditioned by the Democratic Party, the liberal media, and progressive educators to believe that only government can take care of the wants and needs of the people and that the way to show compassion is to appease, coddle, and give handouts.

Good parents love and nurture their kids. They also instill in their children the lessons of life—lessons that will better equip them, when they come of age, to be able to fly out of the nest and thrive. This refers to things like personal responsibility, self-reliance, working for what one wants, and other traits that will increase the odds of success instead of failure. The Democrats seem to want to clip the wings of certain groups in order to keep them in the nest and forever dependent. Look around and see the results of liberalism. You will see minorities living in poverty generation after generation. You will see overly sensitive college students encouraged to run and hide in safe zones instead of being encouraged to learn how to handle adversity. We have seen the women's movement go from "I am woman, hear me roar! I am just as capable as a man to do a job and want opportunities to prove it" to the progressive liberal who shouts "I am woman, hear me whine, and just give me stuff because I am a girl." You will also see those in the upper class get richer pushing this agenda of false compassion, which keeps others down so they can gobble up the bulk of the wealth for themselves. This is the same upper-class establishment that gives out just enough perks and promises to their rank-and-file voters to keep them continuing voting Democrat in hopes of getting more perks thrown their way.

These political opportunists convince their victims—I mean their voters—that the only way for them to get ahead is through government. They convince their victims—oops, I mean their voters—that only government can right all the wrongs, get even with the rich, and make things fair and equal for everyone. The reality is that the bigger the government, the better it is for the political establishments in both parties and their upper-class friends, because they maintain all the control, money, and resources while keeping the rest of us in our place.

In this past 2016 election, millions of Americans rejected the ideas and plans of the Democratic Party and the rest of the political elite to grow government and control us all. We shouted loud and clear that we don't need or want the federal government telling us who we are, deciding what causes we have to support, what health care we have to have, and what values we have to believe in and live by. We shouted loud and clear that we want freedom from the village of the Democratic Party and the rest of the political establishment and their plans for us. But on the other side, millions voted for the Democratic Party and government control. Indeed, this past election proved we are a divided nation.

So how do both sides start to work on getting what they want? Well, I will tell you. It is with states' rights, and we conservatives hope President Trump will lead us in that direction. We have fifty states, and within each state, we have counties. We all don't have to agree and support the same things. Let's agree to disagree and stop allowing the politicians to waste so much of our money, resources, time and effort fighting each other in the attempt to mold us into a one-size-fits-all society. Most of us can agree that we all want what is best for everybody, but we don't have to agree on what that is or how to go about it. We do worry for those of you who are dependent on government and see no need to break away from that dependency. We conservatives believe that people will be far better off if they learn to believe in and depend on themselves more than government bureaucrats. But again, for all you who want to continue to grow government so it can provide for you, we conservatives want you to have the right to pool your money together and grow your state or local government so it can provide for you. We wish you well. Just stop trying to force those government bureaucrats on the millions of us in this country that want to limit the power and control government bureaucrats have over our lives, our freedoms, and our opportunities to provide for ourselves. Thank you for listening, and God bless America!

****************************PSA***************************

Groupthink

Those who make their living in politics, particularly the so-called progressive liberal Democrats, love to ignore the individual and lump us into categorized groups. For instance, they talk about women as though we are all the same. They assume we all have the same issues, wants, needs, and desires. They stereotype women and offend those who don't fit into their profile because they claim to speak for all women, though they don't. Millions of women are independent and want to remain that way. They don't want or need the government to put them into a categorized group that is based solely on their gender and then decide what is or is not important to them.

Women are not the only ones the Democratic Party and other big-government types lump into a one-size-fits-all group. They lump the blacks into a group, the Hispanics into a group, the LBGT individuals into a group, and on and on. They even lump people into groups based on the year they were born.

Conservatives believe it is wrong to lump people together into groups based their gender, color of their skin, sexual preferences, or whatever and then assume everyone in that group fits a certain profile that thinks the same and wants the same things out of life. People are individuals, and they should be treated as individuals and allowed to be themselves without the pressures to conform to a group.

It is the hope of conservatives that we can begin to heal our divided nation by not by allowing politicians to force us into one-size-fits-all groups and then have one-size-fits-all solutions to our problems and issues. Millions of Americans resent being thrown into categorized groups defined by the Democratic Party, which claims to speak for all of us and fights for things many do not want or believe in. Our hope is that we can come together and bust out of the groupthink mentality the liberal politicians are pushing us into and begin to let our individuality shine! Thank you for listening, and God bless America!

**************************PSA**************************

It's Not about Controlling Your Uterus; It's about the Baby

The Democratic Party and their progressive liberal supporters work very hard to cover up, ignore, and redirect the conversation away from the actual procedure and aftermath of abortions, but they claim the issue is about women's rights, women's health, and the rights women have over their uteri. They falsely accuse conservatives, and especially Christian conservatives, that we want to control women, take away their rights, and dictate what they can and cannot do with their own uteri. Well, we conservatives and those of the Christian faith want everyone to know that we believe that women have the right to control their own bodies, and that includes their uteri. In fact, that is how we feel about most everything. We believe in individual freedom and free will. The problems start up when people don't own up to their own actions and cause burdens and harm to others, such as in abortions that cause death to defenseless babies. And that right there is why so many people object to abortions. It is *not* the desire to take away women's rights in order to control their uteri, as the Democrats want people to believe; it is because there is a living baby involved that gets hurt and then killed. This is the reason, and the only reason, millions of Americans object to abortions.

The Democratic Party also claims that abortions are necessary in many cases to protect the life of the mother. This is a gross exaggeration because women facing life-and-death situations would normally be in a hospital instead of an abortion clinic. But the biggest and saddest proof that those claims are exaggerated lies is that some babies survive the abortion procedure and are still killed by those administering the abortion.

The Democratic Party and their supporters believe abortions should be allowed on demand without any restrictions. This includes late-term abortions and the legal killing of babies that survive the abortion procedure, as well as the other inhuman practice of just leaving them to die. Most people, thankfully, disagree with the heartless stance of the jackass party, but that does not mean everyone agrees with the total ban on abortions. Most agree that exceptions should be made in the traumatic rape and incest cases. Others think abortions should be banned unless there are actual medical reasons to end a pregnancy. And others believe abortions should be allowed only at the very beginning of a pregnancy.

Whether you believe all abortions should be banned, allowed only under certain conditions, or allowed regardless of any conditions, we need to all understand that this issue is a life-and-death issue. It not only goes against the belief system of millions but also brings out a lot of emotion and angst for many people who have empathy for these defenseless babies in the womb. Therefore, under no circumstances should anyone be forced to support the abortion industry by having their tax dollars pay for the abortions of others. If the Democratic Party and their supporters on this issue want to promote the practice of abortions as a solution to unwanted pregnancies instead of promoting a living child and adoption programs, then they are the ones that need to donate their time and money to the abortion industry and those seeking abortions.

Of course, if more people would practice the art of

personal responsibility, we could drastically cut down on the numbers of women experiencing unwanted pregnancies. We could also cut down on the numbers of unborn babies experiencing painful death at the hands of abortionists. But sadly, the Democratic Party and its supporters who are proabortion are also anti–personal responsibility and advocates of the "anything goes" sexual revolution lifestyle. And when pregnancies occur, the Democratic Party wants taxpayer dollars to pay for the abortions. They ridicule those who believe that sexual relations are special, not to be taken lightly, and reserved for couples in meaningful relationships. They chastise those who recommend anyone who does not wish to have a child be responsible and either use effective birth control or practice restraint. As a result, far too many people view an unwanted pregnancy as an inconvenience and not a big deal. A person can either choose to have the kid or abort it. Well, we fuddy-duddy God-loving conservatives would like to point out that it may not be a big deal for some to get an abortion, but it is a huge deal and has dire consequences to the little baby in the womb. So it is the baby and *not* the desire to control a woman's uterus that is the reason so many are against abortions and are advocates for pro-life adoption programs and personal responsibility. Thank you for listening, and God bless us all.

****************************PSA***************************

Gay Marriage

One of the big lies pushed by the progressive liberals in the Democratic Party is that Christian conservatives want to prevent same-sex couples from loving each other. The truth is that as long as you don't hurt anyone else, most of us don't care what you do or what your lifestyle is. And we don't understand why you liberals have to get in our faces and make us change our traditions, customs, values and beliefs to accommodate you instead of establishing your own customs and traditions. Be creative, and stop changing the meanings of things like marriage, which was defined by God centuries ago as a union between a man and a woman. Come up with your own term for same-sex unions and leave God's definition alone. But that is not the goal of the Democratic Party and their liberal accomplices in our schools and in the media. The goal of the left is to attack and tear down traditions and values that are based on Judeo-Christian beliefs that have come from God. These liberal progressives are using the federal government and the courts to replace God's ways with their ways.

Another lie the progressive left pushes relates to Christians who wish to reserve their rights to not be forced to participate in activities that go against their religious beliefs, such as baking a cake for a same-sex wedding. Liberals say the refusal of some Christians to provide services for same-sex couples is done out of hate. This, of course, is not true and is in fact done out of love. Christians are a loving, caring people who are truly concerned about the salvation of others. Christians who refuse such services do not want to participate in something they believe may be detrimental to their salvation or the salvation of others and goes against God's plan. It is important to note that Christians believe it is their duty to encourage people to learn about God and follow his word, but it is not our Christian belief, nor is it our desire, to force others into Christianity and make them follow the word of God. It is highly suggested but is not forced on people, unlike the policies of the Democratic Party and that other religion the left makes excuses for.

Conservatives hope that in the future we can all better understand and tolerate each other's beliefs and values even though we may not always agree with each other. And being inclusive should also include those with Judeo-Christian views, values, beliefs, and traditions. Thank you for listening, and God bless America!

***************************PSA***************************

The Failures of Political Correctness and Appeasement

Appeasement and political correctness are two surefire ways of keeping a problem from ever being solved and allowing those problems, issues, or circumstances to grow into dire consequences. Whether done to avoid conflict or done by design for political reasons in order to redirect conversations away from the real problems and solutions, the results are always the same. The problems are not solved and grow worse.

Radical Islam is one of those issues that has grown strong under the shadows of appeasement and political correctness, and it has had dire consequences for millions around the world. We cannot even have a serious conversation about, let alone come up with a strategy to rid ourselves of, these radical Muslim terrorists without the appeasers and political correctness zealots coming out on every news outlet to decry the mistreatment of the Muslim community and their religion. The appeasers claim we must understand these radical groups and that if we show them we mean them no harm, the terrorists will leave us alone and we can avoid conflict. As for the political correctness fanatics, they attack all those who attempt to sound the alarm about radical Islam and claim that attempts to raise such awareness is offensive to all Muslims. So the result is that fewer people are willing to stand up to terrorism in fear of being labeled as people who hate the Muslim religion and its people, which allows radical Islam to rejoice and continue to grow in strength.

This situation is very sad and very frustrating to those who want to fix this problem once and for all because while all this appeasing and political correctness is going on, more women and little girls are captured, raped, and killed by these radical extremists. More gays are being thrown off buildings and killed because Islam forbids homosexuality. People are being put into locked cages and burned alive. People are locked in cages and submerged in water so all inside will drown. More and more people are randomly maimed and killed in terrorist attacks in and around our cities. And more and more people are brutally murdered by having their heads chopped off for the crime of not pledging allegiance to Islam and Sharia law.

The truly frustrating thing is that if the political correctness fanatics, appeasers, and those in the peaceful Muslim community would be as quick to condemn and attack the actions of radical Islam as they are to condemn and attack those who refuse to make excuses for these radicals, we could begin to solve the problem. The political correctness militants, appeasers, and the peaceful Muslim community should strongly denounce these radical Islamic terrorist groups and join the fight against them. But they won't! They claim to be fighting against Islamophobia. But if they really cared, they would want to wipe out Islamic terrorism as much as the rest of us because it is the actions of these Islamic radicals that are causing Islamophobia in the first place. The solution is getting rid of the radical Muslims that are killing people. Then the terrorist acts would stop, the atrocities would stop, and Islamophobia would die. Appeasers, all Muslims, and political correctness fools need to realize that the flames of Islamophobia are being fanned by the actions of Islamic terrorists and not those of us fighting to stop them.

Hopefully we can now recognize the pitfalls of an appeasement strategy and the nonsense of political correctness so we can move forward to rid the world of the death and destruction that is caused by radical Islamic extremism. Thank you for listening, and let's all pray for a peaceful tomorrow.

****************************PSA***************************

Benghazi

The handling of the tragic events surrounding Benghazi is one of many glaring examples of the irreconcilable differences millions of Americans in this country have with the Democratic Party and their leadership. The actions of the Democrat leadership before, during, and after the terrorist attack in Benghazi troubled millions of Americans and confirmed their belief that we, the people, need to be protected from the Democratic Party and that no American should be forced under their jurisdiction against their will.

Repeated requests for extra security by the people at the embassy in Benghazi were denied by the Democrat-run administration at the State Department. The people in the embassy knew that trouble was brewing and were pleading for extra security. But that security was denied by the Democrat-run administration. Then, when the embassy was attacked, their pleas for help were ignored by the Democrats in charge. The trained forces in the area rushing to answer the calls for help at the embassy were shocked when they were told by the Democrat leadership to stand down. Hours later, after our dying ambassador was dragged through the streets, four Americans dead and our embassy destroyed, the Democrat leadership and their liberal friends in the media began the cover-up story.

First, Democrat officials told the American people that nothing unusual was going on in the area to indicate an upcoming terrorist attack, but that it was a spontaneous protest over a video that got out of hand. The Democrats then attempted to frame a guy that posted an anti-Islamic video online and turn him into a scapegoat in hopes that would close the matter. This has now all been exposed as a one lie after another. The Democrat administration knew the area was volatile before the attack, they knew the attack had nothing to do with a video, and they knew Islamic terrorists had attacked the embassy and killed four Americans.

Many Americas wanted to know why the Democrat leadership denied the repeated requests for extra security at the embassy in Benghazi when the government officials knew trouble was brewing in the area. Even more Americans wanted to know why the people in the embassy while it was under attack were abandoned by the administration and their desperate pleas for help were ignored. Many Americans want to know why the Democrat leadership told the forces in the area rushing to help defend those in the embassy to stand down. And many Americans want to know why the Democrats lied and tried to cover up what went on in Benghazi with a phony video story.

Thanks to investigations, we now know what went on in Benghazi, despite the best efforts of Democrat politicians and their liberal friends in the media to stonewall the investigations, mock those trying to uncover the truth, and push the story aside and bury it. As far as the Democrats and their liberal media supporters were concerned, we were supposed to close our eyes and not see that the Democrat leaders denied extra security to those who desperately needed it. We were supposed to turn our heads and not focus on the fact that the desperate pleas for help from our people under attack in a foreign land were ignored by the very people whose job is was to protect them. And we were not supposed to question why the Democrat leaders told the forces on the ground to stand down and not go to the aid of those crying out for help. Then, in the aftermath, we were just supposed to bury our dead and accept the lies we were being told by the Democrats, because at this point, what difference does it make.

While we now know what happened in Benghazi, we still don't know why the Democrat leadership abandoned those at the embassy in their time of need. We also don't know why they lied about what caused the attack, and the Democrats won't tell us the truth. It could be that the Democrat policies were intended to downplay any threats of attacks by Islamic extremists and to cover up any Islamic involvement if there were attacks, in order appease Muslim communities and the rich Muslim countries that contributed huge chunks of money to Democrat campaigns. It could also be because the attack happened right before the 2012 elections and the Democrats wanted to cover up the attack so as not to counter Obama's campaign message that he had the terrorists on the run. Either way, the actions of the Democrat leadership regarding Benghazi are just more of many reasons why no American should be forced under the jurisdiction of Democrats against their will. And with a limited federal government, states' rights, and power with the people, no American citizen will be. Thank you for listening, and God bless America!

****************************PSA***************************

Safety Nets

Conservatives believe in using safety nets to catch those going through hard times and then working to get them back on their feet so they can support themselves, their families, and their own lifestyle choices. The Democratic Party, on the other hand, believes in safety nets that support people for years and years while they depend on others to pay for their needs and lifestyle choices. The Democratic Party does not care about people as they claim. They enable people and allow them to take advantage of the system at other people's expense. If they truly cared about people, they would want to see as many people as possible on their feet and making their way in the world instead of living the life of a kept pet, dependent on its master. The Democrats would also see, if they cared, that there are people truly in need of long-term care and not getting all they need, because of the many able bodies depending on government for their wants and needs, sucking up the resources.

The crossing over the line from helping people to enabling them is just one of many differences between conservative Republicans and liberal Democrats. Conservative Republicans want to be free and independent, and we want to live our lives as we see fit. We want to be as self-sufficient as we can and help others to do the same. The progressive liberals in the Democratic Party think they know what is best for us all and want government to be in charge and have the people dependent on government for their wants and needs. So they are more than happy to have people dependent on government. The more people there are who are dependent on government, the happier the Democrats.

Those who wish to be under the jurisdiction of an all-controlling government that will take care of wants and needs should be allowed to do so. But understand that there are millions in this country that want no part of that kind of government. Conservatives want to be free and independent. And we want to live under a limited, less intrusive form of government that handles things like disaster relief, infrastructure, and foreign affairs but does not try to micromanage the lives of the people.

So how do both sides come together? Easy, we come together, agree to disagree, and honor states' rights. With a smaller, more limited federal government and more power to the states, both sides can get more of what they want. With states' rights, those areas wanting to live under a dominating Democrat-run government can pool their money and resources together to pay for all their programs and services. Then the areas of freedom-loving conservatives that want to be independent from a controlling government run by Democrats can make their way without the burdens of supporting liberal causes and their aftermath. And moderate areas can be moderate.

Conservatives hope we can all agree that the time has come for politics to stop tearing us apart. We don't all have to agree on everything, and we should embrace our differences. We should wish each other well and accept that not everyone wants the same things out of life, and neither side should force its will on the other. If we can do that, we will truly be the United States of America. Thank you for listening, and God bless America!

***************************PSA***************************

Government and Big Business

The left side of the political aisle loves to bash big business. Democrat politicians routinely blame big business for all that is wrong with the world and promise to crack down on big business and their greed once they are elected. Of course, this is all talk—a lot of hot air and empty promises— because in reality Democrat politicians and big business work hand in hand. And the bigger and more powerful the Democrats grow the government, the more it helps their big business buddies. How it works is that people in big business fund the political campaigns of Democrats and establishment Republicans, called RINOs, in exchange for favorable regulations that will help their businesses once they get elected. These regulations help big business get bigger and richer while hurting the smaller businesses and limiting their chances of succeeding because they don't have the money the big businesses have in order to comply with all the regulations the government demands. Therefore, the rich get richer while the poor get poorer. The bigger government gets, the wider the gap between the haves and the have-nots. And the more these elitists use government to take more control over our daily lives, the more the very things that have given the average person the opportunities to better his or her lot in life dry up.

The election of President Trump upset the world order of the Democratic Party and the establishment elite because he could not be bought. We conservatives want to continue to break up the political establishment and their alliances with big business by making it harder for them to keep their power over the people by limiting the power of the federal government and restoring the bulk of the power back to the people and their states. This will put a big stick to the big business / big government power structure and break it up in order to keep the power and control out of the hands of the few at the top and give it back to the people. Those states that want to remain within the big federal government power structure that is pushed by the Democratic Party and political establishment, and the counties within those states, can remain. And the states and counties that want to limit the control such a bureaucratic nightmare has over their state can be free to preserve their power for we the people.

Now, for those who think states' rights and power to the people are new concepts, think again. They are as old as this country's founding, but the federal government, under the leadership of the Democratic Party and the Washington establishment, sucked the power and control away from the states and the people. And the more the feds pulled control away from the states by promising to take care of the people, the more the federal government grew and the average citizen's opportunity to achieve his or her American dream faded away.

Millions of conservatives think it is time to restore the power back to the people and their states, and limit the power of the feds. We vehemently oppose being forced to live under the rule of a one-size-fits-all federal government. We want America to continue to be the land of the free and the home of the brave. And we hope and pray that President Trump and his administration will continue to hear our voices. Thank you for listening, and God bless America!

***************************PSA***************************

Capitalism

Today I want to talk about capitalism. Under a capitalist system, the people own and control their businesses, instead of the government. The government is laissez-faire under a true capitalistic system, which means government politicians don't get in the way and interfere with the people trying to do their jobs and make a profit. Capitalism gives the people the freedom and opportunities to work for a business or to start their own business. Either way, capitalism is where dreams can come true because it is an overwhelming fact that capitalism has given more people who were not born with silver spoons in their mouths the opportunities to make good lives for themselves and their families.

Unfortunately the average American has been living in times when dreams and opportunities have been drying up for everyone except for the upper-class elites in our society. The establishment types in government, led by the Democratic Party and their rich elite friends, worked very hard to replace capitalism with federal government control. Oh, it was great for the government politicians in the establishment and their upper-class cronies because they had already made their way. They just wanted to ensure their money and power stayed in their elite circle by shutting the door on the rest of us. These Democrat politicians and RINO Republicans tried to throw out the freedom of laissez-faire capitalism and use government to pass rules and regulations that helped to grow the businesses of their rich buddies and eliminate the competition of smaller business because they did not have the money or resources to keep up with all the new government requirements and demands. Small businesses were being hurt and even put out of business because they were struggling to keep up with all the red tape and regulations that were being forced on them by the overbearing federal government.

Millions of Americans knew this was happening and felt helpless to stop it. So what did millions of Americans do? They rolled the dice and elected Donald Trump in hopes that he would break up the power structure of the establishment and return the opportunities of capitalism back to the people. With the election of President Trump, the forgotten and left-out Americans have hope once again that they can achieve their American dreams. Thank you for listening, and God bless America!

****************************PSA***************************

The System Is Rigged

"The system is rigged and unfair!" cry the Democrat politicians. "Rich Americans have stolen their way to the top, and we will make them pay their fair share once we get elected!" So says the party of the jackass. During every election cycle, the Democratic Party makes grandiose speeches about how the system is rigged in order to benefit the few at the top while oppressing the poor, the middle class, and, especially, minorities. Well, the Democratic Party would know, because they played a big part in rigging the system and have used every unscrupulous means to do so in order to fulfill their greed for money and power. These ruling-class establishment types in the Democratic Party who are blaming others for rigging the system are the very people who are guilty of doing the rigging so they can grow the federal government and their own personal power. You heard me; the Democratic Party and their rich donors, with the help of the establishment types in the GOP, are the very ones guilty of rigging the system in order to benefit themselves and their rich cronies.

One way these corrupt politicians have been rigging the system for themselves is by shutting down the opportunities of capitalism for the people and replacing it with a powerful federal government run by the political party establishments.

These charlatans convinced their voters that capitalism has failed the people. But in reality, it is the Democratic Party and the rest of the big federal government types that have failed the people. They sold us out. Many have made their riches in the capitalistic system and are now using government to shut the door on the rest of us. These elites are constantly working to grow the power of the government in order to retain their upper-class status and wealth while keeping us commoners in our place by destroying the opportunities of capitalism and replacing it with socialism.

Thankfully the election of President Trump upset the establishment's plans and we now have a chance once again to replace this all controlling federal government with a smaller, less-intrusive-on-our-lives government and open the door to capitalism for the people once again. We can go a long way in achieving this goal by returning the power of the feds back to the states. This was more or less how this nation ran in the past, when it was thriving. Of course, not all areas thrived. There were areas that elected Democrats, and only the areas where the wealthy Democrats lived thrived, while the poor and middle-class areas run by Democrats mostly saw decline. And as the Democrats grew in power and started working with the establishment types in the GOP to find compromise and common ground, more and more areas got neglected while the areas of the rich became more exclusive and wealthy. The Democratic Party did indeed try to take over our government and was working side by side with their big business buddies to rig the system in order to benefit the top percent, while shutting out the rest of us and shifting the blame of a rigged system on others in order to cover up their greedy ways.

We conservatives are truly baffled as to how so many voters still fall for the ruse of the Democratic Party every election cycle. We are also baffled by those who saw what was going on and realized how corrupt the Democrat-run government was but did not seem to care because they got some kind of perk from the government or were in their circle of friends. Either way, those who wish to continue to put the Democratic Party in power because they promise to fight for you and give you stuff, go ahead. But don't force their rule on the rest of us in this country that want to return the bulk of the power back to the states and with the people. Thank you for listening, and God bless America!

***************************PSA***************************

America: Love It or Leave It

Most have heard the expression "America: love it or leave it." I think that expression has become misunderstood because too many people look at America in a certain way and think all others who don't see America as they do should leave. We all need to be reminded that the beauty of America is that it is different and it allows people to be different from one another. We allow ourselves to have different dreams, values, lifestyles, and ambitions. And if others don't like what you say or believe, that's okay. It does not matter if others don't like your ways or beliefs or what you say, because you have the freedom in this country to define yourself and make your way your own. As long as you don't physically hurt the lives and property of others, you generally have the freedom to be yourself in this land. But this is not what is happening in America today. We have too many people in this country that are demanding others change their values, speech, traditions, and ways in order to accommodate others in an effort to fit us into a one-size-fits-all society.

Of course, this has led to a lot of fighting, hurt feelings, and division among the people of this nation. All this fighting and division is not the fault of the people. It is the fault of those in politics, along with their helpers in the liberal media and in our schools, who are attempting to define our speech, values, beliefs, and the one-way direction of the country. These liberal politicians, media personalities, and educators have not only helped the Democratic Party sell their narratives to the public but have also actively supported those who attempt to censor, shout down, demonize, and eliminate from being heard any voices that have different ideas or disagree with anything the left says or does. They say things like "Together we are stronger." Well, that sounds good, but in reality it is anything but good, because they are attempting to force us into a world of one-size-fits-all solutions, ways, and thoughts. These Democratic Party elites, along with their supporters, have pushed the American population further away from their personal freedoms and into conformity—a conformity that is defined and regulated by the Democratic Party bureaucrats using the federal government and our courts.

The 2016 election proved that millions in this country wanted nothing to do with the Democrat politicians, the liberal media, and Washington bureaucrats' plans to control them through government and that they would do anything, including electing Donald Trump, to stop their government takeover. This past election proved that there are millions of us in this country that don't want establishment politicians from either party to tell us who we are, determine how we should think, or tell us what health care we should have, what causes we have to support, what values we must live by, what traditions we can and cannot have, and so on. This past election proved that freedom still rings in America; and if you want a ruling class to replace freedom, then maybe you should leave. That is what that expression "America: love it or leave it" means. It is not "My way or the highway"; but showing the exit door to those trying to deny others the freedom to go down the many highways of life. Thank you for listening, and God bless America!

**************************PSA*************************

Shifting the Blame

Democrats love to shift the blame in order to cover up their past and present ways so they can present an image that they are the party that cares about people. Take the Confederate flag, for instance. The Democrats fight to ban the Confederate flag to show the world they care about black people. They say the Confederate flag is all about slavery, which is not true. What is true is that the Democratic Party in their fight to preserve slavery tainted the Confederate flag. The Democrats should have agreed with the Republicans and freed the slaves and fought only for states' rights. So in actuality, the Democrats, along with those asinine white supremacist groups, should apologize to blacks, leave the flag alone, and ban themselves instead.

The names of sports teams are another thing liberal

Democrats attempt to shift their own guilt upon. Then attempt to show they are the party that cares by trying to force these teams to change the names of their mascots. Take the name "Redskins," for instance. It was picked by sports teams to portray characteristics that it wanted to be associated with. Teams saw American Indians as being tough, brave fighters. So it was a great name for a team and was meant as an honor. Then along comes a group of liberal Democrat activists to say these mascot names are calling the Indians savages and therefore are offensive. Well, most everybody, including Native Americans, see these mascot names as conveying the honor they were intended to and don't find them offensive. But what Native American Indians do find offensive and heartbreaking to this day is that their ancestors were forcibly removed off their land by the government run by the Democratic Party that passed "The Indian Removal Act". Yep, you heard that right. The same Democratic Party that wants to get elected so they can grow the powers of the federal government in order to gain control over the people, their health care, their money, and all our resources because they know what is best for everybody, is the same party that took control of Indian land and forced the Indians to move to other locations. And their reasoning for taking the land from the Indians back in the day was that they knew what was best for the Indians and how to better use their land. This is the same argument the Democrats use today to take away our freedoms and replace them with government control. The Democratic Party still thinks they are the smart ones and they know what is best for everybody. So if they want your land, your freedoms, or whatever, the Democratic Party wants the right to take these things because they feel they know what is best for the common good.

The Democratic Party and the establishment RINOs are just like the politicians of yesteryear. They want to force "we the people" into their common ground box and claim it is for the common good because they are the smart people who know what is best for us all. Well, we conservatives believe those who want to continue to put their faith in the Democratic Party because they fight to ban flags and names of team mascots should be free to do so. We conservatives just don't want Democrats and their policies forced on the millions of us that want no part of their rule.

Restoring states' rights and limiting the power of the feds will help all sides get more of what they want. We as a nation need to come together and agree to disagree. Then we must reject the voices that want to whittle away at our choices and freedoms in order to force us into their one-size-fits-all common ground box because they think they know what is best for us all. Thank you for listening, and God bless America!

**************************PSA**************************

Redefining Words

Democrats are constantly redefining words and their meanings in order to portray themselves as something they are not in order to fool the public. Take the word "liberal," for instance. The word "liberal" generally is thought of as having a sense of anything goes, openness to new ideas and opinions, broad-mindedness, and tolerance of views differing from traditions. And all that is just fine. But the Democratic Party that calls themselves liberals are anything but broad-minded and tolerant of anyone who does not agree with them, traditional or otherwise. They are aggressively hostile to anyone that does not agree with their views, visions, policies, or efforts to gain control over the federal government so they can inflict their will over the people and ban everything that exposes them, challenges them, or threatens their power and control.

Conservatives are also on the list of things the Democratic Party and their liberal accomplices in the media are working to misrepresent and redefine. These liberal Democrats have worked hard to redefine conservatives into something they are not in order to drive people away from conservatism because those on the right believe in limited government and personal freedom, which are in direct opposition to the dream of the Democratic Party. Their dream is a big federal government that they and their elite circle of friends control and benefit from. They never want the people to see what is truly in the hearts and souls of conservatives, so they portray us as something we are not by calling us racists, haters, bigots, xenophobes, misogynists, and any other unflattering term they can come up with.

Conservatives want everyone to know that the vast majority of us are not what the Democrats and their liberal media accomplices say we are. We want the best for everybody, and we believe what is best for everybody is not the Democratic Party and their policies. But because we conservatives believe in freedom and are tolerant of the views of others, we have no problems at all if progressive liberals want to elect Democrats to run the show in their areas. We just don't want the Democrats and their policies forced on us. And with a limited federal government and states' rights restoring the power back to the people, both sides can come together and live in harmony because we will be united in our freedom instead of being forced into common ground conformity that only keeps us fighting and divided. Thank you for listening, and God bless America!

**************************PSA**************************

Let Freedom Ring

There is a political party out there that is salivating to run things for everyone because they think they know what is best for everybody. It is the same political party that moved the Indians off their land back in the day because they thought they knew what was best for the Indians and how to better use their land. I am talking, of course, about the Democratic Party. These Democrats want a powerful federal government that dictates to the people and controls them. Forget the fact that they ran Detroit into the ground to such a point that Detroit is fighting to recover even to this day. And forget the fact that they were in charge of overseeing the water in Flint, Michigan, or that their party leaders and their big-money supporters are filthy rich, living lavish lifestyles while they preach to their clueless voters that they are going to get even with the rich and make things equal. *Ha!*

Then there is another group that wants no part of those eggheads in the Democratic Party that think they know best. We are conservatives, and we want to have a limited government so the people control their own lives and make their own choices. We are the freedom-loving souls that don't want to be forced into a government-run village. We think things run best when people are taught skills and personal responsibility so they will be equipped to support themselves and not be dependent on government politicians for their wants and needs.

This is nothing new, by the way. It goes back to the founding of the country. Settlers came to America in the first place to start a new life and get away from government oppression. As the colonies grew, the king of England began asserting his control over them. It was these efforts to force the colonists to live under the rule of the king that were the catalyst of the American Revolution. And there were colonists then that rejected individual freedom and wanted to live under the rule of the king.

We need to stop fighting each other and recognize that there are those who want to live under government rule and there are millions who don't. Let's come together in this nation and celebrate our differences and let freedom ring. Let's come together in this nation and reject the politicians who claim we must come together and be the same. We are not the same, and we should not be forced by government to be the same. Let's let freedom ring with the preservation of our Constitution, a limited federal government, states' rights, and power to the people! Then those wanting to live under the thumb of government can pool their money and resources together and do so, and those wanting out from under the thumb of Big Brother can thrive with a smaller government that is less intrusive in their lives. Then we can unite as one under the umbrella of freedom that rings throughout our land. Thank you for listening, and God bless America!

***************************PSA**************************

Supreme Court

There are nine Supreme Court justices that currently make up the US Supreme Court. There are also more than three hundred million people in the United States. It is important to know that some political leaders and their supporters are working very hard to stack the deck of the US Supreme Court with liberal ideologues so the court and their rulings can be used to override the will of the people, their votes at the ballot box, and even our Constitution. This was never the intent of the Supreme Court—or any other court, for that matter. But like most things in politics, our courts have been corrupted and turned into power-grabbing tools.

Our courts were never intended to be used as activist courts. But sadly, many courts have been turned into activist courts by liberal Democrats who appoint like-minded liberals to the court and then work to get agenda-based cases in front of those courts, where those liberal judges make rulings designed to force the entire nation of over three hundred million people to adhere to that ruling. Conservatives, on the other hand, work very hard to elect judges that are not judicial activists and respect our Constitution. Conservatives want to appoint judges to the court that will make rulings on a case-by-case basis, adhere to the Constitution, and not use those cases as a means to pass new laws that over three hundred million people will have to live by.

The Constitution of the United States never intended for a room full of judges to have all the power. And the fact that liberal Democrats, with the help of some rollover RINOs, attempt to misuse our judicial system to push their agenda down the throats of millions of Americans is just one of many reasons why so many in this country are fed up with the Democratic Party and establishment politicians.

Limiting the size and power of our federal government, preserving our Constitution, and returning the bulk of the power to the people and their states will go a long way in ending the corruption and power grabs of those in the political establishment and the Democratic Party. Once we restore the power back to the states and with the people, no American will be forced against his or her will to live under a corrupt, out-of-control federal government and their activist courts. Thank you for listening, and God bless America!

****************************PSA***************************

The Beauty of States' Rights

One of the beauties of states' rights is that it allows more choices for the people—choices on how the people want to live their lives and be governed. Areas can be conservative where government oversight is limited, individual freedom is coveted, and personal responsibility is expected. And there can be progressive liberal areas supported by the Democratic Party, where there will be a village, because they believe it takes a village. And in the village, the government decides what is best for the people in the community as a whole, and the people look to government politicians to take care of their wants and needs. We can also have moderate areas, where moderates attempt to appease the liberal side and agree to compromise and water down their desired ways in order to accommodate the left and find common ground. Then the liberal Democrats in those areas, after each compromise, will come back for more concessions until the moderates are beaten into total submission.

Whichever area you want to reside in, we Americans need to agree to stop allowing the political establishment elites in the Democratic Party and GOP to use our federal government and courts to push us into a one-size-fits-all world. We hope and pray that President Trump agrees because people are not all the same. We have different beliefs, values, and desires. We want different things out of life and live in different ways. Of course, your way can't be allowed to physically hurt others and their property; but other than that, we should let our differences be.

We the people need to reject all those in politics, in the media, in entertainment, and in our education system that attempt to push us into their one-size-fits-all federal-government-run society. We the people instead need to come together in the spirit of divided power and states' rights so more choices will remain available to the people. Conservatives need to recognize and accept that there are people who want to live in the government-run village. Liberals need to recognize and accept that even if they perfected their village to utopian standards, we conservatives would still want our freedom from it. As for the moderates, learn to go ala carte. Determine what you want and don't want in your areas and find common ground with the rest of the moderates, but let liberals be liberals and conservatives be conservatives. Think of all the time, money, and resources we can save instead of wasting it fighting each other. Liberals can now reserve their time, money, and resources to perfect their areas instead of spending millions fighting conservatives. Conservatives can use their time, money, and resources as they choose instead of being forced to support things they don't believe in and fighting liberal Democrats. And the same thing can be said for the moderates.

The glue that has held us together as a nation since its founding is not, nor has it ever been, a powerful federal government; it is our Constitution. And it is the efforts of the Democratic Party and GOP establishment types to grow a powerful federal government in order to rule over the people and force us all into their common ground box that is tearing us apart. Thankfully the Democratic Party and the GOP establishment both suffered defeat at the ballot box during the 2016 election. And we conservatives hope the people will continue to reject those in politics that seek to restrict our freedoms in an effort to regulate us into conformity. Thank you for listening, and God bless America!

Reinforcing Trickles
for Conservatives

Those planted segments laced throughout our current mainstream that are designed to make the masses lean toward the left's ways of thinking are what I am referring to as trickles. And all the points the liberals are making with their planted trickles can easily be countered with trickles of our own. We have very creative people on the conservative side. It will be no problem for them to work conservative points and zingers aimed at the left into their work. And as long as we fill our mainstream media and entertainment positions with talented people who believe in conservative principles and Judeo-Christian values and stay up to speed on the antics of the left because they listen to conservative talk radio, we won't need to have coordinated efforts in our mainstream media so everyone will know what points to make in order to fight the left. We can just sit back, let nature take its course, and enjoy watching what our fellow conservatives come up with to counter the left while they entertain us. I, for one, am looking forward to being entertained by personalities other than Hollywood liberals who hate my guts because I don't march to the beat of their phony liberal drum.

The biggest challenge for our mainstream creators will be not to overdo it once there are more conservative-friendly formats that will seek out and highlight the projects and talents of conservatives. Each project, show, or whatever must always guard against sounding too preachy or having their trickles become a tsunami, thus losing the targeted mainstream audience, who basically just want to be entertained. It is also worth repeating that repetition is the key in getting our points to stick into the minds of the mainstream crowd. So it is important to continue to make our points with these ever-flowing reinforcing trickles laced throughout our mainstream, just as the left has been attacking us via the mainstream for decades. And the more conservative-made productions we can get out into the mainstream arena entertaining the public and countering the left, the bigger the impact we will have on the misguided masses.

In getting started, below are examples of reinforcing trickles of some of the more pressing subjects we need to tackle in our future mainstream in order to counter, neutralize, and eventually defeat the mainstream assaults from the left.

Enabling Is Not Caring

The Democratic Party tries and succeeds most of the time in fooling people into believing that they are the party that cares. We need to educate the mainstream crowd that enabling like the kind the Democrats push is not to be confused with caring. An example of a reinforcing trickle to help penetrate into the brain of the mainstream audience that enabling is not a good thing would be a story line in which one character is obviously enabling someone and another character points it out. The enabler says that he or she is just trying to help. The rest of the dialogue goes something like this:

The Challenger: "Are you sure you are trying to help him, or are you just trying to make yourself feel good for trying to do something?"

Enabler: "What do you mean?"

The Challenger: "I mean you are not helping him; you are only enabling him, and that does not help him at all. Plus you are adding hardship to your own life and family. How many times have you and your family missed out on something because you had to bail him out?"

Enabler: "More than I want to remember, but I don't like seeing him go through rough patches."

The Challenger: "He is always going through rough patches because you are always bailing him out, so he is not seeing the consequences of his actions. And because he is not feeling the consequences, he is not doing anything different. He is not learning from his mistakes and learning how to make better decisions for himself."

Enabler: "I just want to protect him. Don't you care about him?"

The Challenger: "It is because I care that I am trying to get through to you that you are not helping him by enabling him. You are treating him like a pet that you take care of instead of letting him learn from his mistakes and grow up. Look, we should always help people who need help when we can, but you need to know the difference between helping someone and enabling him."

The scene ends with the enabler nodding in agreement. This is simple, but done enough times and in enough settings, it will distinguish the differences between helping someone and enabling him or her. And as the Democrats continue to accuse conservatives of not caring because we don't want to pay for liberal causes, our charge will be that Democrats seeking to make themselves feel better are actually hurting people in the long run by confusing enabling and caring. The mainstream crowd needs to see that true compassion is helping people to grow and do things on their own. The masses may never agree with tough-love tactics, but the narrative of the left that coddling people is the compassionate thing to do will be challenged. We must constantly find mainstream ways to point out that when you don't allow people to learn to do things for themselves and overcome the adversities of life, they become less able to cope with life's challenges. Then, to back up our claims, we use footage of college safe zones and liberal freak-outs as examples.

Of course, our biggest weapon in winning this issue will be shielding our side from paying for all the coddled masses while putting the pressure on those who created and promoted this culture of dependency and irresponsibility to finally be held financially accountable and reap what they have sown. And to do this, we conservatives must make it clear to the mainstream crowd that conservatives believe that liberal policies create a culture of dependency because they enable people. Conservatives want to help people be independent and to get quickly back on their feet when they fall because that is what is best for the individual and society as a whole. Then we make it clear to the mainstream masses that halting government funding does not prevent any liberal Democrat from contributing to the causes of his or her choice. And if the liberal supporters of the Democratic Party want to enable people, then they can do it on their own dime. Conservatives believe enabling has a negative effect on people and society. We also believe it is not fair to those who are responsible to be forced to pay for those who are irresponsible. And when we blanket the land with this message in our mainstream and it takes hold, it will be interesting to see how many bleeding-heart liberals will change their minds and drop crusades when they are pressured to financially support their own causes and dependents.

The Ruse of Claiming to Want Fairness and Equality

Once the mainstream crowd sees the blatant hypocrisy of progressive liberal Democrats in regard to their claims that they want things to be fair and equal, the once misguided masses will be just as disgusted with the left as the rest of us. The following skit would be good to run on a future late-night-type talk show to help those in the mainstream crowd that lean toward the liberal side catch up to speed on the hypocrisies of the left.

A Hollywood celebrity is standing in front of her mansion, dripping in jewels and designer clothes, giving a speech to a fawning crowd. In her speech, she states that she believes with all her heart in the Democratic Party and their fight for fairness, equality, and income redistribution. She declares all will be well for everyone once we get 100 percent behind a government run by the progressive liberal Democrats. The crowd cheers, but then a man wearing a suit with a big button in the shape of a rhino steps out of the crowd and shouts, "No!" The man tells the crowd that he is an establishment Republican and then declares the Hollywood celebrity must keep all her wealth and continue to live in her mansion, wear her jewels, drive her fancy cars, and continue to live her life of luxury and forget about all the people who are less fortunate. The Hollywood star declares that is not fair, but the mean Republican snaps back and tells her that he cares only about the rich. And with that, ominous music begins to play. The celebrity sobs to the crowd and declares she tried. Then she turns to go back into her mansion. But then another person emerges from the crowd and informs the people that there are new Republicans in town, and the new GOP denounces the old establishment GOP RINO types. He tells the crowd that the new Republicans are conservatives and they believe in personal freedom, states' rights, and a smaller, limited federal government. Then the new Republican tells the evil establishment RINO to stop standing in the way of rich liberals putting their money where their mouth is. Our establishment RINO knows he is beaten and walks away. Then our new, improved conservative Republican turns to our celebrity and informs her that she is free to give the bulk of her wealth to the Democrats in government so they can redistribute it in the spirit of fairness and equality, if that is what she truly believes in. Our Hollywood celebrity gets a horrified look on her face and swiftly tries to retreat back into her mansion, but the crowd swarms her, and in the next scene we see huge Hollywood mansions shrinking into many little houses. We see a car lot filled with expensive cars transforming into public transportation sites and smart cars. We see country club signs replaced with Open to the Public signs. We see large five-star luxury resorts transform into several two-and-a-half-star motels, complete with average-size pools surrounded by families in lawn chairs. Then, finally, we see a mega Walmart pop up and replace all the shops on Rodeo Drive in Beverly Hills. And while all this transforming is going on, we hear the song "Kumbaya" playing softly in the background.

The skit wraps up with our conservative GOP character telling the audience not to be fooled by rich celebrity hypocrites that support the corrupt Democratic Party, which claims they want to make things fair and equal for everyone because they could do it now if they wanted to and they could have always done it. He informs the audience that nothing has ever stopped any of these rich progressive liberals who support the Democratic Party from pooling all their millions and billions of dollars together and redistributing their wealth equally in their blue Democrat counties. Then he says to the audience, "Beverly Hills and Compton are both Democrat blue areas and things there are not the same. The Hamptons and Detroit are both Democrat blue, so why are the areas both so economically different? Why do the liberal Democrats who live in Malibu, California, have so much more money than those living in Ferguson, Missouri, or Flint, Michigan, when both areas vote for Democrats who claim to want fairness and equality and believe in income redistribution? Why aren't things in Democrat-run areas already fair and equal? Think about it, and stop being fooled by slick Democrat politicians with their celebrity endorsements, and try instead learning how to be self-sufficient so you can stick it to the Democrats before they stick it to you." Then the skit ends.

On our morning and afternoon talk shows, we need segments in which guests come on to talk about the lavish lifestyles and outrageous demands of Democrat political leaders, leftist business executives, progressive tycoons, and liberal entertainment celebrities. This should be followed by a discussion about how they can say they are for fairness and equality yet live the way they do. The segment ends with the hope that more people will be less likely to be fooled by the fair-and-equal scam of the Democratic Party and the rich liberal celebrities who support them. Then we must point out that if these liberals really cared, they would want to help people be independent and make smart choices in life so they would not need to be dependent on government for their wants and needs. It is important to connect the dots for the masses and make a direct connection to the rhetoric of these hypocritical liberals and their actions. By doing so, it is to be hoped, even Democrat voters will be able to spot the hypocrisies and begin to look at all these Democrat supporters not as pillars of compassion but instead as hypocrites and humanitarian frauds.

Then we will need a parade of rude, snarky, rich liberal characters on our shows, portraying these progressive snobs as they are in real life. These show characters should be heard often saying things like "I always vote for the Democrats because Democrats always take care of the rich upper class while fooling the lower classes into thinking we care." And as for all the real-life liberal celebrities with more money than sense, they need to be called upon whenever they do a concert, movie, or some other project to spread their money equally to all the average workers hired to do a job for the event or project. And the same can be said for any liberal-owned business.

As for those rich liberal Democrats touting their charities and good works in the current mainstream media, we need to remind the mainstream crowd that the rich and powerful people the left claims to despise also give to charities and good causes. We should then point out that the vast majority of all the wealthy give to charities but keep the bulk of the wealth to themselves and their interests. Then we tell the masses what the difference is: the Democrats give their rich adherents a pass and attack only those who do not support the Democratic Party for not doing enough.

Lastly, we will need endless reminders in our mainstream about how much money the Democrats spend and waste on things other than making things fair and equal for their rank-and-file voters. This can be done in a variety of ways, from talk show segment topics to a simple reference between two characters in a show where one says to the other that he or she can't believe the Democrats spent millions on a failed green project (Solyndra) instead of making sure Flint, Michigan, had clean water. We can have endless scenes like those written into shows because of the overwhelming amount of obscene waste, mismanaged funds, and outright theft that has taken place under Democrat leadership. These little informative scenes slipped into shows, as already pointed out, are one of the tricks the left has utilized to influence the public for years. The only difference is that our scenes will be based on reality and facts, whereas theirs are misleading propaganda at best.

Nothing in Life Is Free

The freeloader section of the mainstream crowd that is always looking to jump on the gravy train needs to be told on a regular basis that nothing in life is free. The goal here is to educate the freeloader crowd that when they don't pull their own weight in life, it puts additional burdens on others to pick up their slack. We conservatives need to inform the give-me-stuff masses that it is not fair to force other people to pay for the wants and needs of other able-bodied people. Nor is it fair to expect other people to do all the work so others can get their goods and services free of charge. It is sad, but a reality, that we need to explain that goods and services do not just magically appear. Others are working to make things happen, and the freeloader crowd needs to be constantly reminded of that. They should also be asked whether they would work full-time hours with little or no pay so that other able-bodied people could get their stuff for free.

Then we conservatives need to use our future mainstream to serve notice to all the able bodies that want others to pay for their wants and needs, telling them to pressure the millionaires and billionaires who support the Democratic Party and push these entitlement policies to cough up the money in order to pay for all the benefits they promise their voters. Skits and scenes like the one below will help us to educate the misguided masses that liberal ways put burdens on others. These types of skits and scenes will also show the masses that many of the protesters are the not cool activists fighting for change, as the Democrats want us to believe, but just whiny people who want others to pay for their stuff.

An adult protester living in his parent's home rushes in to gather up his protest signs that demand free college for students. On his way out to the protest rally, he pauses to ask his mom what she thinks about the cause. The mom replies that nothing in life is free and she does not think it is fair for people to be forced to pay for the expenses of others. Then she points out that there are many, many, many millionaires and billionaires who support the Democratic Party and their push for these types of liberal causes and programs, such as free college. She also points out that academia is overwhelmingly run and by liberals who support the Democratic Party. She tells her son that she thinks the numerous millionaires and billionaires who support the Democratic Party and these causes need to come together with the protesters and, as a group, pay for everyone's college education if that is what they want to do. Then she adds, "If liberal teachers want to teach for free to help lower the costs, they can do so. And if liberal celebrities and Democrat politicians want to give speeches at schools for free instead of charging the school a hefty fee for their words, they too can help the schools lower costs so the savings can be passed on to the students."

Then Mom goes on to tell her son that while they are on the subject of nothing being free, because someone else always has to pay the cost, there are the added expenses she incurs for him to live under her roof. She suggests that since he has time to protest, he should have time to get a job and start helping out with household expenses in order to take his burden off of her shoulders. The scene ends with the son standing in stunned silence.

Scenes and skits like the above running in our mainstream will counter the left's narrative that benefits and entitlements are free. Someone has to pay, and our right-wing position should be that if the liberals want to pool their money together and pay for all the promises they made to their voters, they are free to do so. And when they balk—and they will—we will just keep pointing out all the millionaires and billionaires on the liberal side that want to force others to pay for their causes via government taxes and adding to the national debt while they sit on piles of cash. And when they say we don't care about people, we will inform them that we believe in the strongest possible terms that it is best for all individuals and society as a whole for all able-bodied people to be independent and support their own lifestyles. We will also state that we believe in the strongest possible terms that creating a culture of dependency like the left does is cruel and harmful to a person's development and society as a whole. Again we will use all footage of abject poverty in liberal-run areas, along with liberal freak-outs on college campuses, as examples to support our statements.

It is important to note that the goal here is not to get the liberals to pool their money together to pay for all the stuff they promise. They don't have enough money, and in fact, the whole country does not have enough money. But the liberal and, sadly, RINO establishment path is an out-of-control national debt and our nation crumbling within. So we conservatives must put a stop to the practice of buying votes that is growing government, bankrupting our country, making dependents out of our people, and establishing a ruling class. To do this is to pit the freeloader crowd against the wealthy liberal Democrats and compromising RINOs by highlighting their outrageous hypocrisies in mainstream formats while putting pressure on them to pay for their own political promises out of their fat-with-cash pockets. This will make the rich donors of the Democratic Party and RINO elite think twice before supporting the entitlement agenda if they are going to be put into a spotlight and called upon to put *their* money where *their* mouth is. Right now, the current liberal mainstream covers for them. But when our conservative mainstream drowns out their mainstream, the hypocrites will have no place to hide.

The Myth of White Privilege

As with all the other idiotic liberal talking points, this one will be easy to throw back into the face of the left. In addition to one-line zingers and scenes in shows that point out the absurdity of white privilege, we need to post, in areas where the misguided masses will see it, footage of Hollywood celebrities and New York socialites living the good life during the 1930s. Then, along with that footage, we need to post footage of the hordes white people waiting in lines to get food during the depression. We need to directly challenge the left's narrative of white privilege with clip after clip in our mainstream programming that shows the suffering and hardships of whites all through American history, and then contrast them with clips of Hollywood stars and New York elites. We must take every opportunity, when presented, to point out that Hollywood and New York elites are the ones of privilege today and yesteryear. And they are the very same privileged East Coast and West Coast types that voted for the establishment queen in this past election.

Those doing talk show-type news and entertainment for our mainstream need to routinely go out and about to ask the average working American a series of questions on the topic of white privilege. Those segments need to start out with a montage of liberal talking heads accusing white people of having white privilege; then the segments jump to interviews of white people doing nonglamorous jobs. In the interviews, the host will ask these people about their white privilege and whether it bothers them that liberal egghead teachers, Democrat politicians, and wealthy liberals in the media are saying that they are privileged because of their whiteness.

Then the liberal media talking heads—especially those who push the white privilege narrative while making an income white middle-class Americans can only dream about—need to be shown a mirror. These overpaid liberal hacks in the media need to be called out as the ones leading privileged lives, and we need to let the misguided masses know that we conservatives think those hacks should be ashamed of themselves for falsely accusing a whole race of people of having a privilege that they themselves have. And again the segments should show pictures in mainstream formats of whites all throughout American history up to the present struggling and working to make a living. Then those pictures should be contrasted with the media talking heads saying that all whites have privilege, while they sit in their anchor chairs having someone touch up their makeup while another is bringing them their cups of coffee. Then the amounts these talking heads are making should flash on the bottom of the screen, and then that salary should be contrasted against the average salary of white middle-class Americans doing less glamorous jobs.

It is important to connect the dots for the masses by pointing out that those who push the narrative of white privilege are liberal Democrats who fall into two groups of people, the first being those who have the privilege and want to keep it by electing fellow liberal Democrats who will preserve their elite status while making the masses think they are fighting for them. The second group consists of people who have been bought off or fooled into believing the rhetoric of the jackass party.

Conservative America and Hispanics

As of this writing, we are being bombarded with immigrant sob stories, and we need to counter with stories that show and tell the other side, such as a scene in a show where the breadwinner of a family lost his or her job to an immigrant and was forced to train the replacement. These scenes need to show the fear and worry that real families go through. Then we should follow up on our future mainstream-type conversation shows that invite guests on to tell their real-life stories of going through personal hardships due to Washington's refusal to secure our borders. In addition to those stories, we should tell of the loss of lives of both American citizens and many immigrants themselves due to dangerous immigrants coming into this country and committing violent crimes.

Then, to counter the charge that immigration laws break up families, we should show how liberal policies of the Democratic Party break up families with scenes that depict sad farewells between families and friends when their loved ones are forced to move away from their homes in order to find opportunity. We will show friends and families sadly moving apart from each other because of the lack of economic opportunities in their Democrat-run areas after Democrat policies dried up opportunities for the average citizen in poor and middle-class areas while paving the way for their cronies in the rich establishment areas to suck up the bulk of the wealth. But in addition to telling the stories of families forced to move from their homes to find a job, we will also tell the stories of families torn apart by tragedies caused by rampant violence in Democrat-run areas due to the lack of economic opportunity and liberal appeasement of criminal behavior. And in each one of these stories, the finger needs to point squarely at the Democratic Party as the reason for the families being torn apart.

We also need reinforcing trickles to dispel the notion that anyone against open borders and sanctuary cities hates Hispanics. Conservative Hispanics that understand how America was founded and want to be a part of that America need to be front and center in our mainstream programming to explain to the bleeding-heart masses that not all Hispanics agree with the left and do not want to be political pawns for the Democratic Party but instead desire to be self-sufficient legal Americans. To help accomplish this, we will need little snippets that can be slipped into any show regardless of the main plotline of snarky liberals coming into contact with conservative Hispanics. In these chance meetings, a typical liberal cause could be brought up, such as open borders. Our snarky liberal could spout out the latest leftist talking point, only to be surprised when they are shot down by our hero, the conservative Hispanic, who informs the liberal that he believes in a strong border and is against amnesty. I know this sounds simplistic, and it is, but those little reinforcing trickles, done in enough different shows on a repetitive basis, will get into the psyche of the mainstream audience and will begin to dispel the narratives of the left.

We conservatives need to make sure the mainstream crowd and all Hispanics understand the differences between being a liberal pawn to achieve the Democrat dream or wanting freedom and opportunity to achieve the American dream. And we need to make our points with a steady flow of public service announcements, skits, songs, videos, plotlines in shows, jokes, zingers, talk show segments, and the rest of the mainstream ways in order to reach the misguided masses. And once we reach that section of the mainstream crowd and turn the left's useful idiots into informed citizens, the only remaining idiots that will vote for the Democrats will be the liberal ideologues.

Reinforcing Trickles
Addressing LBGT People

The left-leaning masses need to see that there are many in the LBGT community that don't like all the political correctness when it comes to their sexual choices; we're just fine with civil unions and do not like the militant left's attack on Christianity and traditional marriage. We need to showcase gays and lesbians that denounce the tactics of the Democratic Party and don't want to pressure others to denounce the word of God.

In addition to LBGT conservatives coming on to talk shows to tell their stories, we need scenes like the ones below in our future shows to begin to quell the hatred that has been ginned up against Christians and conservatives regarding the LBGT communities. We need to show the LBGT folks and the rest of the mainstream crowd that Christian conservatives do not wish to harm anyone, try very hard to have love in our hearts, follow the teachings of the Bible, and that is it. Our mainstream needs to present Christian conservatives as they are in order to counter the image painted by the left that we are no-fun, backward, crazy people who hate. And once we begin to dispel those images, more and more people will begin to gravitate toward Christians, Christianity, our churches, and God. And that right there should be the goal in our mainstream media when it comes to Christianity, as opposed to the left's wish of having people recoil from Christianity and dump God's ways for their ways.

A good example to begin to dispel the narrative of the left and clear up misunderstandings regarding LBGT people is scenes like the one below, between two parents and their gay son, being written into entertainment shows. The dialogue goes something like this:

Gay Son (to his parents): "You must love me, not judge me, accept me for who I am, and support me with all your heart and soul. You people need to get with the times, denounce what the Bible says, and start supporting the gay and lesbian movements."

Straight Parents: "We do love you; we don't judge you, accept you for who you are, and support your rights to be who you are. We support the rights of all people to be who they are. We are not, however, going to support the movements, because we love you."

Gay Son: "How can you say it is out of love that you won't support the movements? Don't you know it hurts peoples' feelings when you don't support gay and lesbian lifestyles?"

Straight parents: "It is because we have love in our hearts and genuinely care about our fellow human beings that we are not going to support anything that might adversely affect one's salvation. Now, whether you accept that or not is up to you. Whether you are going to judge us for that is up to you. And whether you are going to stop loving us and denounce us is up to you. But we would like to remind you that tolerance is a two-way street. Intolerance is a one-way street. Because we want to be tolerant, we are not going to demand you denounce anything you believe in, as you are demanding of us. We are also not going to demand you support what we believe in. Now, we ask you, are you going to love us, not judge us, and accept us for who we are?" The scene ends with a puzzled look on the gay son's face.

Another scene features two lesbians arguing over gay marriage:

Lesbian 1: "How can you not support gay marriage when you are a lesbian?"

Lesbian 2: "I will admit that I wrestle with what the Bible says about homosexuality, but that does not change the fact that I believe in God. I believe he loves me and wants what is best for me. And I am sorry if it makes you upset that I don't support gay marriage, but the Bible says that marriage is between a man and a woman, and to push gay marriage just to stick it to Christians is not what I want to do."

Lesbian 1: "Gay marriage is not about sticking it to Christians. It is about our right to love each other."

Lesbian 2: "Oh please, you can't fool me about what the agenda is in the LBGT movement. You know as well as I do that the vast majority of Christians and conservatives don't want to pass laws that prevent anyone from loving whoever they want. They just want to follow the word of God and preserve the meaning of marriage as being between a man and a woman, as was defined by God centuries ago. So to say the movement is about love is a lie, and you know it. It is all about tearing down the traditions and beliefs built around Christianity. So if you want to chastise me because I am a lesbian that does not support gay marriage, then so be it, and we can stop being friends right now!"

Lesbian 1: "No, I don't want to end our friendship over this. I guess I am the one that needs to be more tolerant; and you are right, the LBGT movement is more about sticking it to Christians, their traditions, and their beliefs than it is about love. I guess I should have already seen that because they totally ignore Islam for believing the same thing and just go after Christians."

Lesbian 2: "Yes, that is true. But let's change the subject and decide where we are going for lunch."

Lesbian 1: "I agree; let's go eat." The scene ends with the two women walking away while talking in a friendly manner to each other.

Now, scenes like the above are not going to change the minds of the militant left, but who cares. They are not our target audience. Our target audience is all the people who bought into all the lies of the left that Christians are haters that want to pass laws that keep people from loving the adult of their choice. And the reason they bought into that lie is because it was overwhelming what those people heard in the liberal-controlled mainstream. It was also pushed hard in the schools, but more on the schools later.

It Is Not That You Are Black; It Is That You Are Likely a PODP

Mainstream talk shows hosted by conservatives to promote our conservative talent are a must. As we all know, liberal talk shows are used to sway opinion, and we must do the same with ours to correct the many lies told by the left. One of these lies is that most white conservatives want to keep blacks down and are racists. So an excellent series of skits to run on one of our future late night talk shows about once or twice a month is a series of skits with the topic of "it's not that you are black; it's that you are likely a product of Democrat policies [PODP for short]".

Here is an idea I have for presenting such a series: The host of one of our future late-night-type talk shows starts out telling the audience that it is no secret that many blacks think white people are racist because the Democratic Party tells us they are. They tell us that white people lock doors when they see a person of color, walk to the opposite side of the street when they see a black coming, and are hesitant to get on an elevator or share a cab with blacks. Then the host expresses his desire for the races to finally come together by explaining the real reason for the great divide—and it has nothing to do with skin color but has everything to do with the politics of the Democratic Party. Then the host tells the audience that the show will be introducing a series of skits with the theme of "it is not that you are black; it's that you are likely a PODP" to help him get this point across. He then informs his audience that "PODP" means "product of Democrat policies" and that it is no secret that the vast majority of blacks vote for Democrats and live in communities run by Democrats. Then the host or hostess tells the audience that these skits are not designed to offend but are an effort to achieve a better understanding between the races and to get everyone to have an enlightened awareness regarding the actual cause of the problems that exist between the races. Then the first of many of these types of skits begins.

A smaller-than-average white man pushes the button of an elevator. The elevator opens up, and a large black man is alone in the elevator. The white man pauses, and the viewers hear his thoughts. He is distressed that there is a black man in the elevator because everyone knows most blacks believe what the Democratic Party tells them, as the majority of blacks vote for Democrats. (Then a bubble of actual footage pops up with Hillary screeching about slavery, then a bubble of Obama accusing all whites of having white privilege, and another bubble with Biden saying whites want to keep blacks in chains.) Again the viewer hears his thoughts. He does not want to be alone in an elevator with someone who probably hates him because he is white. Then, all while the man's thoughts are being heard, a comedy element can be added while the little guy squirms as the black man on the elevator stares him down. Then our little guy takes notice that the man on the elevator is holding a set of the Rush Revere books written by conservative Rush Limbaugh and is relieved to know the man is a fellow conservative. Then the smiling white man boards the elevator and greets the black gentleman with a friendly hello. The skit ends with the elevator opening up on another floor and the two exiting while talking happily to each other. Then a catchy little tune starts to play, and a narrator reads the following like a disclaimer in a drug ad: "The fact that blacks are black and whites are white is not the driving source of division between the races. It is that most blacks are Democrats and a product of their policies. Democrats want blacks to think it is their skin color, but it is the politics and rhetoric of the Democratic Party that fuel the friction and prevent harmony between the races. So it is not that you are black; it is that you are likely a PODP."

It will be a constant stream of lighthearted skits like the

above, in addition to harder-hitting segments in our other programming that highlight the destruction liberal policies have had on the black community, that will eventually begin to chip away at the left's hold over black people. And to further put a nail into the Democrat's coffin, we should constantly shame the Democratic Party, the liberal media, and the liberal educators in our mainstream programming for putting hate in the hearts of so many people with their calls of racism instead of looking at how their own failed policies, political rhetoric, and slanted reporting of incidents involving the police as the real reasons for the struggles in liberal-run black communities.

The Myth of Democrats Being the Champions of Women

The Democrats' claim that they are the champions of women is another myth for us to disprove. And as with all the other false narratives of the left, there is an abundance of material to prove the liberals wrong. However, our mainstream media won't bury the evidence, as does the mainstream of the left. The mainstream crowd needs to be introduced to accomplished conservative Christian women. The whiny masses need to see accomplished conservative women that own their own businesses, run companies, run their households, make top salaries in their chosen professions, or, the hardest job of all, raise kids. These liberal activists and their supporters need to know that they are a source of embarrassment for conservative women and that the only path they are paving for women is a path of dependency on government. Again, the best way to the heart and mind of a clueless Democrat voter is through a skit, talk show segment, or story line in a movie or television show. So, in addition to conservative women coming on our future talk shows to inspire other women to succeed and to avoid falling into the male-bashing victim status that is pushed by the Democratic Party, we should have scenes written into shows that go something like this:

> An old hail-damaged Prius runs into the back of a new luxury vehicle in the parking lot at a mall. As the woman driver of the Prius gets out of her vehicle to check the damage, she notices the other driver is a woman she went to college with over a decade ago.

Prius Owner: "Hello, long time no see. Sorry I ran into you, but everything looks okay."

Luxury Car Owner: "That's good. How have you been?"

Prius Owner: "Not so good. Still trying to make it in a man's world. But I am still protesting the system and fighting for women's right's just like we did in college. How about you?"

Luxury Car Owner: "Oh, I am doing great! Instead of protesting for women's rights, I was out doing, and now I am the owner of my own company and doing very well. I found out that it does not matter if you are a man or a woman in the business world; both have to deal with adversity, both can fail, and both can make it big. And speaking of making it big, I've got to run. I have a big meeting in thirty minutes about our latest success, and I don't like to keep my employees waiting. It was good to see you."

> The luxury car owner rushes off and leaves the owner of the old hail-damaged Prius to slowly walk back to her car. As she gets back to her vehicle, she pauses to look at her protest signs demanding equal pay for women in her back seat and then looks toward the road to watch her friend drive away in her new luxury vehicle, and the scene ends.

This type of scene could be incorporated into most any series by having a show's regular female character be influenced by a liberal protester and start hanging out with her. Then, after meeting an accomplished, successful woman, the show's character dumps the protester and aspires to be more like the independent, successful woman.

Another good scene to have in our mainstream is a liberal woman screeching about women's rights on a street corner and being confronted by a woman wearing stylish business attire who tells the protesting woman to stop speaking for all women. The rest of the conversation goes like this:

Protester: "I have to speak for all women because we are being oppressed and it is time for our equality! It is time for us to have our rights! It is time for women to be in control of their own bodies!"

Businesswoman: "Well, stop it. I don't want you to speak for me, and there are millions more women just like me that wish you would stop claiming to speak for all women."

Protester: "Don't you want to stop being oppressed by a society that wants women back in the kitchen, cooking dinner for their men? Don't you want to have equal rights and equal pay? Don't you want to have control over your own body?"

Businesswoman: "Look, I am a woman that started out with humble means, and now I am making it on my own. I have two brothers that started in the same circumstances, and I am making more money than they are. Women are not being oppressed, and we have all our rights. And it is embarrassing for millions of women like me to be associated with women like you who are making fools of themselves protesting for things women already have in this country while wearing knitted cat hats and carrying profanity-laced signs. And we have control over our bodies, but if we use our bodies to harm ourselves or other human lives, then society should step in. Now, with that said, please stop claiming you are speaking for all women, because you are *not!*"

Protester: "Well, statistics show that the majority of men get paid more than women!"

Businesswoman: "Well, maybe if more women would spend more time looking for and taking advantage of opportunities to grow and advance in life than they do protesting in silly knitted hats, then maybe those statistics would improve. I am living proof that women can make just as much as or more than a man doing the same job in a company. I make more than my male coworker because I am better at my job, not because the government made my employer pay me more just because I am a woman. I earned my salary, and that is the way it should be."

Protester: "Our hats are not silly, and you are offending me."

Businesswoman: "Well, you offend me by claiming to speak for all women, so I guess we are even. Hey, that means we are equally offended! We reached equality!"

Protester: "You are just making fun of me and the movement now! You are offensive and a misogynist."

With that the businesswoman starts to laugh, the protester storms off in anger, and the scene ends.

Of course, the big fight that gets the liberal women riled up the most is the right to abort a baby. The left has successfully managed to make the term "abortion" synonymous with "women's rights." I bet you could ask any woman that gets her information from the liberal mainstream media to define "abortion," and she would say that it is a right women have to control their own bodies and that evil right-wing forces are trying to take that right away from them. We need to counter that by making the term "abortion" synonymous with what it is—killing a baby. And to do that, every time we talk about abortions, we should not use the word "abortion" but say "killing a baby" or "the right to kill your own baby." When liberals say women have the right to get an abortion, we say the liberals want the right to kill their babies. When liberals say that not allowing abortions is taking away from women's health care, we counter by pointing out that if a woman's health is in danger, she needs to be in the hospital and not in an abortion clinic killing her baby. When they say conservatives don't care if women are forced into back-alley abortions, we say we don't want anyone to go to a back alley to kill her baby. Then we suggest adoption as a safer alternative to the mother and the baby. And when they shout slogans like "My body my business," we simply counter with "Bodies should not kill their babies."

Another powerful tool is the amazing images we have of babies in the womb. Our future afternoon-type talk shows should have segments in which doctors come on to show those amazing images of babies moving around and sucking their thumbs. Then the medical guest should be asked to describe in detail what happens to babies at various stages of development if their mothers decide to terminate their lives. And as the doctor is describing the horror the babies go through, the cameras should show the disturbed faces of audience members. That is one of the basic formulas of swaying public opinion the left has been using on us for decades, and it's time they got a taste of their own medicine. We are probably not going to change the minds of the rabid feminists, but they are not our target audience anyway. If we can reach the misguided masses in the mainstream crowd to think of abortion as what it is instead of as a right, the days of thinking abortions are no big deal will be over.

Now, I know some are thinking that we have already

exposed what goes on in the abortion industry to the public and people still don't care. But I will counter that we haven't done this in the world of mainstream news and entertainment. It is not our fault, because we have been shut out by the progressives that control most media outlets. But today is a new day, and when conservatives compete and then defeat the liberals in the world of mainstream news and entertainment, stories of mailing baby parts through the mail and what went on in Dr. Gosnell's clinic will hit the mainstream instead of just being discussed in conservative circles. Once that happens, attitudes about abortions will change.

The Environment

Oh, the hypocrisies of the left regarding the environment that are routinely exposed in conservative media circles, with talk radio programs leading the charge. Transforming these gems into mainstream formats and turning the mainstream Democrat voter's attention to these hypocrisies will be especially rewarding.

One excellent movie idea or series of skits would be for true-blue global warming believers to be elected to power and start seizing all of the assets of the rich liberals in New York and Hollywood in order to buy solar panels for every home that is occupied by people making less than $60,000 a year. The environmentalists demand all the Hollywood stars and New York elitist sell their mansions and live in just one modest home. Then they are pressured to sell their cars (even their electric ones) and take public transportation to save energy. The environmentalist leaders also chastise the

Hollywood industry for making entertainment for people to sit and watch. They claim that making entertainment shows contributes to global warming and that resources could be saved if Hollywood stopped production and encouraged people to take walks and exercise as a healthier alternative to sitting down to watch their entertainment. Then the climate police accuse the Hollywood elite of not only contributing to climate change but also promoting couch potato activities that lead to obesity.

Then the environmentalists go after the high-end fashion world and claim the designers are wasting resources and call for a one-size-fits-all uniform for people to wear. Then they chastise the elites in the world of fashion for using vital resources, making clothes that not everyone can afford. Then finally the environmentalist go after the Democrat Party and the wealthy donors that support them as the worst offenders and crack down on their elaborate lifestyles and wasteful habits. This idea could be made into a comedy, drama or both. But either way there needs to be scenes where the liberal elites try without success to explain to the militant environmentalist that all the global warming stuff was a ruse to get Democrats elected so they could get access to the money and power so they could make even more money by forcing people to buy green products under the guise of saving the planet.

Another idea that would attract the attention of the mainstream crowd is a celebrity global warming hypocrite of the week. Shows and websites could even work together to select the winner of the week. Then the winner could be showcased on all the participating websites and shows to expand the audience base. And all the potential candidates' past and present hypocrisies should be considered and exposed in the process of picking the winner for the week

My favorite tactic would be directly asking the celebrities that support global warming if they feel guilty about using more resources than the average person for their mansions or for having more than one home, as well as for their many flights or other modes of transportation they utilize that they claim contribute to global warming. Then we should ask whether the houses and travel are more important to them than saving the planet. Even if they say they have to travel for their job, we can counter by asking if their job is more important to them than the planet. Now, there are two reasons to do this. One reason is to expose their hypocrisy to the masses in hopes that they will lose their credibility and ability to use their fame to sway public opinion. The second reason is to make the global warming hypocrites think twice before they shoot their mouths off and support liberal causes just to get accolades from the current mainstream progressive press.

Then, finally, we should point out all the money that has been made by some pushing global warming hysteria and making green products under the ruse of saving the planet. Many have become massively wealthy as a result of the global warming racket. So as we are using our mainstream to expose their hypocrisy and wealth to the masses, we conservatives lead the charge and challenge these global warming hypocrites to alter their lifestyles and learn to live permanently with modest means so they can use their millions and billions to supply green products to the masses for free. And when they don't do that, or when they donate just a small portion of their wealth as a show, we conservatives will use all our media outlets to point out that if they really thought global warming was going to destroy us, they would not be so stingy with their wealth.

We Must Never Stop Teaching the Pitfalls of Socialism

There are already many excellent videos out on the web designed to help the masses see the pitfalls of socialism, such as one in which a classroom of students gets the same grade regardless of the work put in, resulting in a riot in the classroom. This is a good one because it is one that many young people will be able to relate to. We just need to get skits like this out of conservative circles and into the mainstream so the masses will be exposed to them.

We also need to showcase the countless examples of how abuse always increases when too much power gets centralized and falls into the hands of a select few. For instance, in Hollywood we saw women endure sexual harassment for decades because the power to work in that industry was held by only those in the clique, centralized in New York and Hollywood. And of course, all the abuse of power that goes on in the swamp of Washington will give us an abundance of material we can showcase as examples of why too much power centralized and in the hands of the few is never a good thing.

Investigating Corruption, Democrat Style

We must have reinforcing trickles placed in our mainstream media to highlight the differences between how the Democrats and the liberal media investigate and cover blatant Democrat corruption, as opposed to their investigations and coverage of them fishing for possible Republican wrongdoing so they can blow every little possible scenario out of proportion. For instance, we need to have all kinds of skits that show groups of egghead liberals investigating a possible Republican scandal. It can show these investigators armed with magnifying glasses, talking to media hacks and making mountains out of molehills about every little thing they see. Then this can be contrasted against their investigation of one of their own in the Democratic Party. In those scenes, the same investigators will have blinders on, and in the background we will see all kinds of suspicious activity going unnoticed. One such activity could be a man stuffing money into his clothes at one of the scenes involved in the investigation. Then, as the investigators report back to the media that nothing suspicious is going on, the liberal media quickly agrees and then switches coverage to the office of a high-ranking Democrat politician, where an interview has been set up to further discuss the matter. The Democrat politician states in the interview that all involved in the supposed scandal are innocent of all wrongdoing and that their honor and integrity are above reproach. While the interview is taking place, we see the man that was stuffing money into his clothes enter the office and begin unloading money from his clothes into a desk. The interview wraps up, and the media talking heads confirm again that there is nothing to see and that no evidence of any corruption by the Democrats has been found. Then the reporters switch the topic to the latest breakup in the celebrity world.

Another good story line or skit for our mainstream would be set in a liberal newsroom. In the newsroom, we see liberal journalists salivating about running a story that hammers a conservative, even though a young journalist working on the same story is informing them that the facts are not adding up. The old liberal dogs are undaunted and are still eager to run the story out to the public. At the same time, a damaging story about Democrats is breaking, and the evidence of their misconduct and corruption is becoming overwhelmingly obvious for all to see. We then see another young, eager journalist in the newsroom telling the seasoned old liberal journalists that he has video and audio of the Democrats committing the crimes, but he is also ignored by the senior members of the progressive press.

As these liberal elites of the press are busy putting together their hit piece on the conservative, the young journalist also working on that story receives a phone call from their only source for the story. After taking the call, the young journalist informs his older colleagues that he just heard from their only source and that he admitted to making up the whole story about the conservative. But the old guard snaps and informs him that it does not matter at this point because of the seriousness of the charge. The young journalist again tells his colleagues that the whole story is untrue, but he is again ignored. Then the other young journalist who gathered evidence of crimes and corruption on the part of Democrats approaches the veteran news anchors and asks them where they want the audio and videos that prove crimes were committed by the Democrats in question. The old guard reporters take the young journalist's evidence and thank him. But the minute the young reporter turns his back, the old guard throws the evidence in a nearby trash can and sets it on fire. Then, as the Jurassic liberal journalists rush to their set to begin reporting the fake news about the conservative to their viewers, we see the fire from the trash can begin to spread through the newsroom. As the liberal hacks finish reporting their hit piece on the innocent conservative, the scene or skit ends with breaking news about a fire in their newsroom, and the liberal journalists report they have credible sources that the fire was started by an extreme right-wing Republican.

Another skit would be the same Jurassic liberal journalists replaying a recorded statement from a Republican politician and trying to find something they can use to damage that Republican. The scene shows the liberal journalists listening to the recording over and over again as they nitpick at every word. Then, when they fail to find something they could use to hammer the right-leaning politician, one of the liberal hacks suggests they play the recording backward to see if they can hear something sinister. So the eager group plays the recording backward and listens very intently, but sadly, nothing is heard. The group, refusing to give up on the opportunity to make a Republican look bad, starts to work on the possibility of saying that some of the words used in the statement could be code words with hidden meanings. As they begin work on those possible scenarios, a young journalist runs in with a recording of a politician caught making a heartless statement about not caring if a patient has cancer. This news makes the old liberal guard ecstatic, and they rush to get that statement out to all their media outlets so the public will boil with outrage at the uncaring, mean politician. And as they gather with smiling faces, giddy with anticipation, to listen to the evil statement of the heartless politician saying he did not care if a patient had cancer, their joy quickly turns to sadness as the statement is played and they realize the statement was made by a Democrat. The scene ends with the Jurassic liberal journalists yelling at their young colleague as they throw the recording of the Democrat into a nearby trash can and set it on fire. We can even use fictitious names for our Jurassic liberal news characters, such as Christopher Fakehews, Larry Lyingopolus, and Pandrea Bitchell.

Entertaining the masses and challenging the left's authority in the world of news and information while steering those who want to know more about the events of the day toward conservative talk radio and true conservative nonestablishment news sources should be the goal of our conservative mainstream. The current liberal mainstream news media is filled with Democrat hacks that the mainstream crowd looks upon as the voices of reason and authority. And the only reason the mainstream crowd looks at the liberal hacks as the voices of reason and authority is because that is what the liberal mainstream media and entertainment industry tells them. But when we get more conservative-made entertainment out into the mainstream—skits and scenes like those above that show liberal journalists in the unflattering light that they deserve—the credibility of the liberal mainstream will start to get even more tarnished in the eyes of the mainstream crowd. And in addition to making fun of them in scenes and skits, we will also give them a taste of their own medicine by describing them in our mainstream as the real controversial extremist kooks. Then we can inform the masses in our programming that the true voices of reason and authority are nonestablishment conservative news reporters, sites, and conservative talk radio personalities like Rush Limbaugh. When our mainstream is in a position to do all this, the path to conservative talk radio, conservative news sites, and conservative programs will be paved for the masses to follow. And as more and more people get curious and tune in to conservative talk radio and other conservative sites, the vast majority will be hooked because they will see truth and reality about the events of the day discussed for the first time and will grow just as disgusted with the left as the rest of us. Then the liberal dominance in the mainstream news arena will take such a hit that even the RINOs will become less likely to jump on their media-driven bandwagons.

Liberal Democrats Are Not the Cool Kids

The mainstream crowd, for the most part, does not like political correctness but has no clue that it is a product of the liberal Democrats. So we will need reinforcing trickles placed into our mainstream to inform the mainstream crowd that liberal Democrats are responsible for the epidemic of political correctness and are not the cool people they claim to be. They are instead massive control freaks that push for boring conformity among the masses while they attempt to define people, categorize people into groups, tell us who we are, and claim to speak for all.

In order to connect the dots for the masses to see that

it is the Democrats who are the main drivers of political correctness and not the cool cats that they claim to be, we need a series of scenes that can easily be placed into our entertainment shows. These scenes should show a random conversation between two strangers that occurs when a liberal overhears another person making a comment that they perceive as being politically incorrect. These conversations will always be overheard by a third party that will agree with the conservative point of view and will irritate the liberals because the third party will be originally perceived to be on the liberal side. And those scenes will go something like this:

A rather small-framed woman walking in the park passes a white man talking on his phone. She overhears him making a comment that she perceives as racist. She decides to follow the man, and when he finishes his phone conversation, she calls him a racist. Another man, who happens to be black, passes by when she does this and hears what she calls the man, so he stops dead in his tracks. The rest of the dialogue goes like this:

White Male Victim: "What did you call me?"

Liberal Woman: "I heard you on your phone describing someone named Roger. You said he is black and needs to be on a short leash whenever you go out with him in public. Then I heard you laugh. That is a racist thing to say and is offensive."

White Male Victim: "I bet you are a liberal Democrat?"

Liberal woman: "I am. How did you know that and what does that have to do with you being a racist?"

White Male Victim: "I thought you might be a liberal Democrat because you were quick to pass judgment on me and call me names even though you have not one clue what is in my heart or how I truly feel about things."

Liberal Woman: "Well, what you said was racist and offensive!"

White Male Victim: "Well, it is offensive to me to be judged and called a racist by someone who does not know my mind or heart but instead nitpicks at how I express something, in order to pass judgment on me and slander my character. I wish liberal Democrats would take more time to learn what is in a person's heart instead of nitpicking people apart, looking for something to be offended about. Oh, and by the way, Roger is my dog."

With that being said, a black gentleman that has stopped to listen says, "Amen to that." He then high-fives our white male victim.

Liberal Woman (to Black Gentleman): "How can you agree with him?"

Black Gentleman: "Well, little lady, I agree with him because it is true. Most people who point their fingers at others and call them racist do not take the time to know what is in a person's heart and mind before they pass judgement and call people names—especially liberal Democrats! You can always tell Democrats because they are quick to judge and to call those who disagree with them racists, bigots, homophobes, or whatever."

Liberal Woman (to Black Gentleman): "Well, you are a sexist for calling me a little lady because that is demeaning!"

With that, the scene ends with the two men looking at each other before bursting into laughter and the liberal woman storming off, but not before calling them both racist misogynists, which makes the two men laugh even more.

These types of scenes will have a big impact on the mainstream crowd once we get enough of them out into our mainstream entertainment vehicles. Another type of scene would be an argument between a conservative and a liberal about amnesty for illegals that is overheard by a Hispanic who chimes in to say that he wants a strong border and does not believe in amnesty. The Hispanic then tells the liberal that the best way to help the people of other countries is to create a system in which people won't have to flee their homes and families in order to pursue better lives. Our hero Hispanic further explains that what needs to be done is to challenge other countries to stop suppressing their people with government rule and start showing them the ways of freedom and opportunity through capitalism so that their people can have opportunities like Americans do when conservatives are in charge.

We need scenes in which a liberal is accusing a conservative of Islamophobia because he wants to go after Islamic terrorists. A Muslim man injects himself into the conversation to inform the liberal that his son was killed in a terrorist attack, so he also wants to go after and eliminate

Islamic terrorists. Then the Muslim man rips into the liberal person for helping radical Islam continue their reign of terror by appeasing those who commit atrocities in the name of Islam and attacking those who want to get tough on fighting terror.

Then, of course, we will need scenes in which liberal women are hammering women Trump voters because they did not vote for the first female president, asking "How could you not do that?" And the answer will always be "Because she was a Democrat, and their liberal policies are a disaster." Then the women Trump voters go on to explain that it may be hard for Democrats to understand, but most people outside liberal circles don't care what color someone is, what sex he or she is, or whatever. They go on to inform the disgruntled Hillary voters that most people on the conservative side decide whom to vote for by picking the person they think will do the best job, and that is it. Then the Trump voters turn the tables on these liberal women by suggesting that if all they want is for a woman to be president, let us unite together and nominate a conservative Republican woman for president, allowing women to have a better chance at breaking the glass ceiling. The scene ends with the liberal women calling the Trump voters a bunch of vile names and storming out of the room.

We conservatives can have a field day showing the liberals in their true light for the mainstream crowd. And of course we will need those one-line zingers. A good one would be to show annoying characters being controlling and attempting to force their will on a group of people, only to be called out by other characters to stop acting like liberal Democrats. We can also have characters pointing out that another character is acting like a liberal Democrat because he or she is being a whiny victim that refuses to do things for himself or herself and expects everyone else to come together to carry his or her load.

We also need to have skits on our future late-night talk shows of a group of liberals wearing Democratic Party campaign T-shirts poking repeatedly at a bear and annoying the hell out of it. Then show them crying and saying they were victims of a bear attack when the bear finally hits back. We can repeat that sentiment with scenes in shows in which an annoying character insults everyone he or she comes in contact with and tries to undermine people every way he or she can until finally someone gives the character a taste of his or her own medicine. The audience will then see that annoying character flip out and play the victim. And the scene will end with the other characters saying that the annoying character is obviously a liberal Democrat because he or she can dish it out but can never take it.

Another scene or skit has a group of people eating at a table that take notice of a group of liberal Democrats coming over to sit with them. The group at the table starts to complain and begins to get up to move, but they are too late. The liberal Democrats descend onto their table and immediately begin to dictate to the people at the table what they should and should not eat. The liberals then explain that a committee was formed and they came to a consensus that people should no longer eat certain items. The liberals then look over the table and take items off of the plates of the people sitting at the table. One of the people tries to object, but the person sitting next to them gestures to let it go and then attempts to change the dynamic of the situation by bringing up the nice weather. The liberals quickly object to the conversation topic because not everyone has nice weather as a result of global warming, so therefore any topic about nice weather is offensive. With that, all those at the table sheepishly look down at their plates and pick at their food until another person at the table attempts to bring up an upcoming football game. But no, the liberals at the table shoot down that topic as well because football is a male-dominated sport and is therefore deemed sexist and offensive to women. Then a woman at the table declares that she likes football and she wanted the food they took off her plate. She then gets up and informs those sitting at the table that she is going to go get another plate of food and take it outside to eat it in the nice weather. The smug liberals at the table tell her to go ahead because they did not want to eat with her kind anyway. So the women standing up to leave declares a food fight, and the liberals get pounded with food. The scene ends with the group of nonliberals enjoying their lunch in the sunshine.

Scenes, skits, and zingers like that, along with a steady flow of public service announcements and real-life stories that will be told on our future mainstream talk shows, will destroy the image the left so carefully crafted for itself that they are the enlightened cool kids. And soon the mainstream masses will be rolling their eyes along with conservatives at the name-calling tactics and political correctness nonsense of the liberal Democratic Party ideologues.

Compromise and Finding
Common Ground vs. Freedom

The push to find common ground and compromise by the Democrats and establishment types for all the issues of the day has long been exposed as the power-grabbing political tactic that it is by our more astute talk radio personalities. But to the mainstream crowd, it sounds like the sensible thing to do because they are not exposed to any other alternative. It is always presented to us in the liberal "lamestream" media whenever the Democrats lose elections that compromising to find common ground is what you do and that only crazy obstructionist types question the process. Then all the establishment types jump on that bandwagon, and together they bemoan the notion that if the government can't find common ground compromises, then nothing gets done and it is a disaster for all. When Democrats win, their ways are crammed down our throats while the RINOs remind us that elections have consequences.

In our conservative mainstream, we need to debunk this myth. We need to convey that forced compromise in order to find common ground on most issues is unnecessary and restrictive. We need to keep reminding the masses in our mainstream that we have fifty states and each state is broken up into counties, so we don't all have to do the same things, find the same solutions to our problems, or force everyone to support the same causes.

We also need to look for ways to repeatedly make the point that all the infighting and resentment caused by politics is a result of establishment politicians and the Democratic Party trying to force their rule over us all and not letting our individuality shine. We need to inform the masses that all the angst and despair felt by some after the election of Donald Trump only illustrates the need for a more limited federal government and more power to the people. Then we must inform the masses that coming together and having unity in our country does not mean doing the same things, being forced to believe in the same things, forced to support the same things, or forced to compromise to find common ground when one doesn't have to. We must have constant reminders in our mainstream that the United States is the land whose people are united in the spirit of liberty and freedom. And the more we are forced together in the name of common ground by liberal Democrats and establishment types, the more divided and resentful of each other we become.

Repetition is key in reaching and maintaining influence in the mainstream, and our drumbeat is freedom, and liberty unites us! Forced government compromise and one-size-fits-all common ground restrictions divide us! We conservatives need to shout from the rooftops in our mainstream media that we believe in individuality and reject politicians that try to define us, attempt to tell us who we are, and use government to force the American people into a one-size-fits-all common ground box.

As we are shouting from our rooftops, we need to run scenes like the following in our mainstream programming in order to help the left-leaning spoon-fed masses better understand our point of view by making our points in ways even the politically challenged can relate to:

A man is looking down at his phone outside a dressing room in a clothing store while waiting for his wife, who is trying on some clothes. She comes out wearing one of the potential new outfits and asks her husband his opinion as a group of busybodies approaches. The rest of the dialogue goes something like this.

Wife: "How do you like this one?"

Husband (without even looking up): "It's fine."

Wife: "You did not even look at it!"

Before Husband can defend himself, the group of onlookers interrupts and injects themselves into the discussion.

Group Spokesperson: "We have discussed your outfit and come to a consensus that the belt for that outfit does not work at all. You must lose the belt. The skirt is fine, but we would like you to seek another top to go with it."

Wife: "Excuse me, but who are you?"

Husband (without even looking up): "I bet they are liberal Democrats."

Group Spokesperson: "Well, some of us are and some of us are moderates. Thank you for noticing. But now back to your outfit. We need to make some changes."

Wife: "I like the outfit! And since I am going to be the one wearing it and paying for it, I should decide!"

Group Spokesperson: "Well, we might run across you again sometime wearing that outfit, and we will have to see it. So it is best you compromise and find common ground with us so we can come together and find something we can agree on."

Wife: "How about I pick out and wear what I like. Then, when you go shopping for your things, you can pick out and wear what you like."

Group Spokesperson: "It is best that we compromise in order to find common ground so everyone is happy."

Husband (looking up): "Compromising and finding common ground are necessary in a few cases, but not in most. And it certainly does not make everyone happy. When you force people to compromise their choices away in order to find common ground, we lose variety, the ability to choose different paths for ourselves, and the ability to handle our problems and issues differently."

Group Spokesperson: "But when we compromise, we are coming together. When we are together, we are stronger. And when we find common ground, we are united as one."

Wife: "We are united in our freedoms. Being forced to compromise on things so we can fit into a one-size-fits-all common ground box is not united; it is forced into conformity. And it certainly does not make us stronger! But it does create resentment and in fighting between the people. Now, if you will excuse me, I am going to go buy this outfit."

Husband (finally looking at the outfit): "Looks good; let's go."

The scene ends with the liberal group storming off.

Another skit might go something like this: A couple is moving into a new home when they are approached in their yard by a woman holding a clipboard. The woman identifies herself has a member of the neighborhood and gives the couple a list of social causes she claims the entire neighborhood supports. She goes on to explain that those in the neighborhood are billed fifty dollars each month and that the money is pooled and distributed to these social causes. The couple, after looking over the list, explain that they are just moving in and do not wish to participate but will continue to give to the causes of their choice. The woman with the clipboard says she understands but is insistent they participate because together they can make a difference. And the rest of the dialogue goes like this.

Husband: "Well, I am not sure about some of these causes. I could support a few of them, but not all of them."

Woman with Clipboard: "Oh, we can compromise and find common ground! Just show me which of the causes you can support and cross out the causes you are not comfortable supporting, and we will adjust your payment accordingly." So the couple looks over the list and crosses out most of the items and hands the list back to the women. The woman thanks them and informs them that they will receive their instructions soon on how to make their payments. Then she welcomes the couple into the neighborhood and leaves. After the woman with the clipboard is gone, the couple discusses the list.

Wife: "Did you see all the left-wing liberal causes on that list?"

Husband: "I sure did. They were all on the list, complete with their phony compassionate buzzwords."

Wife: "Do you think all the people in this neighborhood support that list?"

Husband: "I hope not, because if they do, we moved into a liberal Democrat hotbed."

Ominous music is heard as the couple looks around their new neighborhood.

"A month later" appears on the screen. We see the same couple in their new home when the doorbell rings. The couple opens the door to find a man with a clipboard holding the list of causes minus the ones they already agreed to support. The man explains he is there to reach a compromise and find common ground with them on the remaining items on the list of causes the rest of the neighborhood supports. He gives the couple the list and asks them to let him know which items remaining on the list they will support. The couple explains to the man that they did all this a month ago when a woman came to their home with that very list on a clipboard. The rest of the dialogue goes like this:

Man with Clipboard: "That was then; this is now. I am here today to compromise with you in hopes we can find common ground on the remaining items on our list of important social causes. Which items remaining on the list of causes will you agree to support?"

Husband (getting angry): "I am not going to support anything else! I already did this!"

Man with Clipboard: "There is no need to raise your voice. I am willing to compromise and find common ground with you."

The wife, hoping to calm the situation, asks to see the list again and agrees to support two more items. This angers the husband even more but satisfies the man with the clipboard, and he goes away.

Husband (to Wife): "Why did you do that?"

Wife: "Well, this is a new neighborhood, and I don't want to cause trouble right off the bat. I want to fit in and get along with everybody."

Husband: "Remember the causes on that list? They are liberal causes, and you can't fit in with liberal Democrats unless you are willing to agree with them and think like them. They don't want compromise; they want conformity!

They will be back with the same list, and they will keep coming back until they have us agree with everything on it!

Wife: "Let's not get upset about it. Let's hope that now they will be satisfied and will leave us alone."

Another month goes by, and sure enough, another liberal with the same list and the same clipboard comes to the couple's door. And as expected, the liberal asks the couple to support the remaining items on the list but lets it be known they are willing to compromise and allow the couple to select just a few more. But this time the husband excuses himself and leaves while the wife explains that they have decided not to support any of the causes on the list. Then she shouts, "Now, honey!" and shuts the door. As soon as the door closes, the sprinklers in the yard start spraying water. But to the surprise of the couple looking out their window, they see the woman and the man that previously visited their home with the list jump out of the bushes as the water starts to spray. As the couple laughs, seeing the three annoying liberals running from their yard while getting soaked, they also notice the neighbors who live in the houses around them coming out of their homes and applauding. The couple comes to find out that the rest of their neighbors had run the annoying liberals off as well. So the couple fits right in with new neighborhood and lives happily ever after.

So as we are pushing in our mainstream media and entertainment that it is okay for people to be different and that we should let our individuality shine, we must also keep reminding the masses how one-size-fits-all conformity keeps us divided and is not even necessary in most cases. We should also constantly remind the mainstream crowd that when Democrats and establishment moderates win, they want to use the federal government and our courts to force their ways on everybody using compromise and common ground tactics, and that is not right. Then we must point out that when conservatives win, we want to limit the control of government so all sides can get more of what they want by preserving the Constitution and freedom.

Then we constantly remind the masses in our mainstream that nothing is stopping liberal Democrats from pooling their people and resources together and making their liberal utopias work. We also inform the masses that the reason liberal Democrats say things like "Together we are stronger" is because they need others and the money of others to prop up their failed policies because they do not work and soon drain all their resources. We need to tell the masses that it is time for the Democrats and compromising moderates to stop forcing others against their will into the village but instead make their millionaires and billionaires use their money to prop up these failed liberal policies. Then we must challenge Democrats in our mainstream to make their ideas work fairly and equally in their liberal circles and leave the rest of us alone!

Our Own Award Shows

The mainstream crowd loves award shows. But like everything else, the liberals have taken over the award shows and have ruined them for many viewers. Not only do liberals use award shows to spew their venom, but the voters involved in such shows have admitted to voting for projects they have not even seen; they voted for them simply because those projects advanced a liberal narrative. We conservatives need to have our own awards and award shows, allowing conservatives to honor the news reporters, writers, and talk radio personalities that have worked hard over the years to report the news and events of the day accurately to their listeners, readers, and viewers. The nominees and recipients should also be chosen by true conservatives. And once we get more of our entertainment-type movies, programs, and the like out in the mainstream, we can have our own awards for those as well that are voted on by conservatives in that industry. We could even call our award for entertainment the *Duke*, after the late, great John Wayne, who loved America.

The reason we need our own awards is to honor our own that get ignored by the left. The awards will also show the mainstream crowd that millions of people recognize and honor conservatives as exceptional human beings. Awards do give credibility to the people who receive them in the eyes of most people, and when the mainstream crowd sees only liberals honored and conservatives trashed, it hurts us and elevates them.

In Conclusion

Thanks to talk radio, we conservatives can see what the Democratic Party and the rest of the political establishment are attempting to do to the people in this country as plain as day. We can connect the dots, but it is abundantly clear that far too many in the mainstream crowd cannot. So we must use our conservative mainstream media to connect the dots for them so they can see what we see. Think of all the liberal hypocrisy, double standards, corruption, failed policies, wasted money, lies, and on and on and on as little dots on a page. Among rank-and-file Democrat voters, most know things are not right, but they don't see the big picture. They just see all the things wrong, and they have been conditioned by the liberal media and our schools to look to government to fix it. But once we start connecting the dots for the masses in our mainstream productions, the general public will start to see the connection between the problems and the Democratic Party. And just like the coloring books we played with as children in which we connected the dots to see the picture on the page, our mainstream media will connect the dots for the masses. As we proceed, more and more of the misguided mainstream crowd will begin to get a clue and see the true picture of liberalism, as well as the true picture of conservatism and Judeo-Christian values.

That the rank-and-file Democrat voter does not already see these liberal elitists as they truly are is attributable to the current liberal mainstream media and entertainment industry. And it is a glaring reminder that we need to replace the liberals in the mainstream arena. The liberals have used the mainstream media and entertainment industry to define our culture and put it into the gutter. It is time for them to be defeated not just at the ballot box but also in mainstream news and entertainment. Never in my lifetime has the liberal mainstream media and entertainment industry been in a better position to be toppled than it is right now. We on the right must not waste this opportunity! And if anyone doubts me and says that God-loving conservatives do not need to topple the liberals' hold in the mainstream arena because we already have many conservative sites and talk radio getting this information out and because the Democrats lost big in the 2016 election, please take note that over 45 percent of the population in most of the states voted for the Democrats. That is too close for comfort; this is no time to rest on our laurels.

The election of President Trump has given those of us with conservative principles and Judeo-Christian values more time to defeat liberalism and a chance to get our message out to all the people. The liberal mainstream media spews out their lies and propaganda to defeat us on a daily basis. They are vile and are 100 percent against us. They do not deserve to be the mainstream media and entertainment industry in any country, and they need to be replaced.

Prior to the election of President Donald Trump, conservative talk radio fans and those of the Christian faith felt attacked on all sides. The mainstream liberal media, the entertainment industry, the schools, the Democratic Party, and even the Republican Party leadership were all against us. We felt as if we were surrounded and the opposition was going to go in for the kill after the queen was elected. We clung to conservative talk radio and prayed for a miracle. Well, the miracle happened, and now it is time to work like never before and take the mainstream media and our schools away from the left and save our country for good.

THE SCHOOLS

I T IS NO SECRET that progressives have taken over the schools and pushed their liberal agenda on the students, and sadly the results have taken their toll on our youth and society. The liberals would not have been as successful in overtaking our education system without the Democratic Party, teachers' unions and mainstream media working as one for a common goal. And their one common goal was not, and is not, the education of our youth but the indoctrination of our youth to advance the power of the Democratic Party and their leftist agenda.

The liberal mainstream media will continue to back up those liberal narratives as worthy endeavors and heap praise and admiration onto the pushers of liberalism in our schools while attacking those who dare to fight against it. Liberal activists indoctrinating our kids in our schools is a crisis and has been for a long time. Liberals love a crisis, and we should give them one. Once we get enough of our mainstream outlets in place, we need to hit them with coordinated blasts. And our blasts should include every single piece of footage we have of liberal educators making fools of themselves, trashing the capitol building in Wisconsin when they don't get their way, shooting an image of Donald Trump with a water gun while yelling "Die! Die! Die!" in the classroom, making violent, threatening statements at protests, and on and on and on. And with every clip of liberal teachers acting badly, we accompany that footage with the title "Crisis in Our Schools: Who Is Teaching Our Kids!"

Then we point out to our mainstream viewers and listeners that the vast majority of these types of stories involve liberal activists who care more about their political axes to grind than teaching our kids. We need to make heroes out of our conservative warriors who are going into our schools in an attempt to improve the education quality of our kids while pointing out that the Democratic Party, teachers' unions, and liberal activists are the problems. And as our mainstream media heaps accolades on our conservative educators, administrators, parents, and students who are trying to make a difference, more and more will step up to fight liberalism in our schools once they know others will have their back.

Then, in order to make the biggest impact with the misguided masses, we will need scenes in our entertainment programs that show students and parents feeling bullied if they don't fall in line with a teacher's leftist ideology—scenes like a teacher telling his or her students that they need to show up to a liberal-supported protest and that if they don't, it will affect their grade; scenes like a student writing a paper that does not support the teacher's view on global warming and getting an F even though the teacher admits the paper was written well. And in each of these types of scenes, the liberal teacher exhibits the same unhinged qualities as the real-life activists do.

Then, to continue to pile it on, we can also highlight on our future morning and afternoon mainstream-type talk shows real-life frustrated parents who have spent fortunes on college in hopes their kids will acquire knowledge and skills in order to reach their full potential in life. But sadly, their kids returned home indoctrinated leftists because liberal educators spent valuable class time indoctrinating their kids with liberal ideology and causes. And if that is not bad enough, liberal administrators promoted the liberal ideology and left-wing causes on their college campuses while preventing conservatives from expressing their points of view. The result is after all the money spent, their kids are more equipped for protesting to get others to pay for their wants and needs instead of equipped for thriving in life.

We will also inform the masses of the money the teachers' unions take from the paychecks of our teachers. We need to inform the mainstream crowd that many teachers don't agree with the teachers' unions and their liberal ways but are forced to pay dues in order to keep their jobs. We will point out in our mainstream that we hear all the time that teachers don't make enough money yet are forced to give some of what they do make to the rich teachers' union, who then gives it to the even richer Democratic Party. Then we need to have knowledgeable guests on our future morning and afternoon mainstream-type talk shows to discuss how the Democratic Party and the teachers' unions work together to get rich off of the dues of teachers while pushing a curriculum that is designed not to educate our kids but to indoctrinate them with liberal ideology.

Once liberals are exposed for what they are and challenged, they crack, crumble, and call people names as they go down in defeat, which will only give us more ammunition to use against them. So as soon as we can pull out all the stops and expose the liberal activists in our education system as a problem, using scenes in shows, jokes, skits, talk show segments, and hard-hitting news, our education system can get back on the road to recovery and begin to educate instead of indoctrinate.

Now, as we are exposing the liberal loons and the damage they have caused to our education system, we will start a steady stream of reinforcing trickles that praise the kind of education we conservatives want for our kids. Our kids need the kind of education that teaches them useful knowledge and skills so they will have the tools to achieve their dreams in life. And they need to be taught the true history of the founding of this country. Rush Limbaugh has written a series of books for kids that do just that, and the kids love them. Those books need to be in our schools, but of course the liberals will freak out because they are written by Rush. This is where we push back hard in our mainstream and explain that all the provocative things Rush has said over the years were aimed squarely at the liberals. And the reason he said those provocative things about the progressives was to call them out, point out their hypocrisies, and raise awareness about their agenda because he saw early on the destructive nature of liberalism. He knew that they wanted nothing more than to destroy everything about this country he and millions of Americans believe in. We will not back down and will firmly declare that Rush was right all along, that he is part of the solution, and that those objecting to his books represent the problem.

Other things our kids need to start learning again in schools are the traits of success. Success means different things to different people, and whatever a child's definition of success will be, our schools should give them the tools to achieve it. I myself have written two children's books that do just that: *The Kids on Prosperity Lane* and *The Kids on Prosperity Lane Reach for the Stars*. They are short stories for young readers that teach kids about personal responsibility, determination, persistence, believing in oneself amid negativity, decision-making, and setting goals. I believe that when you teach kids these traits at a young age, the chances of these traits becoming habit are much greater. These traits, of course, counter the traits of failure taught by liberals, who condition kids to be dependent on government, to be a victim, and to seek out the nearest safe zone.

We also need to make sure the Constitution of the United States is taught properly to our youth in our public schools. We must make it our mission for all high school graduates to know what the Constitution is and says. They should also know what conservatives believe and why. They should know what capitalism is and what opportunities it offers to the people when it is not reserved for only the few at the top. And they should be taught what socialism and communism are and be shown why neither has worked for the people but has only rewarded the upper ruling class.

It is going to be a daunting task for our conservative education warriors to defeat liberalism in our schools. But it will be, without a doubt, an easier path for them to forge with a mainstream media and entertainment industry that has their back instead of working against them. And that is just another reason out of many why we God-loving conservatives must get up to speed and compete, and then defeat the influence the liberal mainstream has over the people in our country.

HEALTH CARE

REGARDLESS OF HOW THE Trump administration deals with the health care system, all freedom-loving conservatives must find a way to protect ourselves from government-run health care and shield ourselves from the resulting lifestyle regulations and financial burdens. It is the liberal and establishment dream to have the government run health care because of the power it yields over the people. They will never give up, and neither should we. And remember: whatever the government passes, whether it is good or bad, can be undone.

The conservative fight against government-run health care will have a better chance to succeed once we have more mainstream outlets getting our message out to the misguided masses. And increasing our odds in beating back those who want to force government-run health care down our throats is one of the many reasons why it is imperative that we repeal and replace the current mainstream media and entertainment industry. Below are messages we need to convey to the misguided masses once we get our conservative mainstream up and running.

It is not fair to force others to pay for the basic health care needs of other able-bodied people who refuse to carry their own weight in life and support their own lifestyle choices. It isn't fair for those in need to not get the best of care because our resources are strained because too many able-bodied people refuse to support their own lifestyle choices and demand others to foot their bills. It is not fair to force people to pay for the medical procedures of others when those procedures go against their religious or personal beliefs. It is not fair for millions of Americans to be forced into a one-size-fits-all government-run health care system against their will. And it is not fair to deny millions of Americans the abundance of choices the free market can provide for health care and insurance needs.

Now, it is undeniable that the freeloader crowd is a huge factor in the rising costs of health care, but there are other factors. And we conservatives should lead the charge and go after those who price gouge or partake in other activities that spike the cost of health care unnecessarily for their own personal gain. We should lead the charge to go after insurance companies who drop people from their plans once they become sick, or who raise their premiums to unsustainable levels. It is these and other unscrupulous activities on the business side of health care that hurt hardworking Americans and give rise to the calls for government to take over the health care industry. Plus it will annoy the left because they want everyone to believe that only they go after the greedy that take advantage of the sick, even though they were quiet when a Democrat senator's daughter greatly profited from the skyrocketing prices of the EpiPen at the expense of those in need.

As conservatives work with the free market system to improve the cost and quality of health care in America and go after those who gum up the works by milking the system or contribute to rising costs through greed like the

Democrat senator's daughter, we conservatives need to toot our own horn in our mainstream media so the misguided masses will see that it is conservatives that care about keeping health care affordable for all. And as we are tooting our own horns, we must make it very clear to the misguided masses that nothing is preventing liberal Democrats and moderate RINOs from getting together and forming their own insurance company with all their millionaire and billionaire supporters and cover whomever or whatever they want. We should challenge the liberals and establishment types to make their ideas work in the free market without risking taxpayer dollars and forcing people into their plans.

Now, what are we to do concerning insurance for preexisting conditions? We need to explain that it is not fair to those who act responsibly, get insurance, and pay into their plans to have their insurance premiums go up and their medical bills padded in order to pay for those who were irresponsible and did not seek to insure themselves until they became sick or injured. And as for those who did act responsibly but had their insurance cancelled because they had a rough patch or became forgetful as a result of old age and missed some payments, we will take care of those people, and this is how we will do it: If it is found the insurance company dropped coverage using unscrupulous means, we in our mainstream will hammer that company and put pressure on them to reinstate that person. All others, including those who never had insurance, should be allowed to put their medical expenses on a low-interest payment plan, providing the treatment is deemed necessary for the health of the patient. Of course, there are going to be cases where uninsured and even insured people will be facing catastrophic conditions that will cost them beyond their capabilities, and then safety nets funded with our tax dollars will come into play. As for all the rest of the cases, local charities can play a huge role in helping those in need pay their medical bills. Conservatives have big hearts, and we will have more money at our disposal to help those truly in need when we are not forced to pay for the basic health care needs of liberal ne'er-do-wells milking the system, or procedures that go against our values and beliefs.

The states and counties that adopt a low-interest payment plan option should have the discretion to determine which treatments and procedures will be allowed to be charged to these low-interest payment plans and how aggressively they will pursue the nonpayers. And these states and counties should be clear with the taxpayers and the medical facilities in their states and counties on which procedures they will back with taxpayer dollars and which procedures will not be backed, so the facilities and voters can decide what they do and do not want to risk being responsible for if the debt goes delinquent. This will allow more protection for people in conservative-run areas from being stuck paying for unnecessary procedures or for procedures that go against their values and beliefs if their elected conservative representatives are making those decisions.

As long as a medical facility carries the debt, that facility should earn the interest so those in charge of the medical facilities might take some risks and perform procedures and administer treatment not covered by the state or county. But it will be up to each medical facility to decide its guidelines and risks. And of course, in liberal areas, anything will likely be acceptable to their Democrat representatives. But it will be up to the liberal taxpayers in those areas to either foot the bill or vote those out of office that stick them with the medical bills of others getting abortions, boob jobs, nose jobs, sex-change surgery, or their daily pot fix.

It is important to note that the federal government is not involved at all in the low-interest-payment-plan-option idea. And the state gets involved only if a person can't pay for his or her health care needs and expects or needs taxpayer assistance.

Competition in the free market will drive the cost of health care down so people will be able to afford health care that is not tied to their jobs. It is going to be interesting to see if we can get the hands of the feds out of our health care system and get it back into the hands of the people, their doctors, and the states, where the free market and conservative ideas can compete with liberal ideas. Then, in our future mainstream, we can document the success of our ideas in our conservative areas as well as the failures in Democrat-run areas. Of course, not all of our ideas will be winners, but we will keep score! And I have no doubt we will be able to show the masses that, more often than not, our conservative ideas work and the liberal ideas continue to be epic fails for everyone but the upper elite.

BACK THE BLUE AND
ALL LIVES MATTER

I AM WRITING THIS ON Friday, July 8, 2016, the day after police officers were gunned down in the streets of Dallas, Texas, the city in which I was born and live not far from. As I write this, not all the details of the attacks are known. The investigations are just beginning, but this much I do know: the Democratic Party, the current liberal mainstream media, and those in the Republican Party that have appeased these radical leftists are to blame. I blame them more than the shooter because I believe the shooter felt justified in his rage because of the political rhetoric of those in the Democratic Party and the way their liberal hacks in the media report the news. Don't get me wrong; I blame the shooter who carried out these attacks and believe he should never see the light of day again. But the Democratic Party and the liberal media care not a whit that they do not tell both sides of the story and report outright lies that stir up anger and emotions in people. They do it for the sole purpose of advancing the liberal agenda and securing votes for the Democratic Party. Well, last night the Democratic Party's rhetoric and their left-wing reporting in the mainstream media ginned up enough anger and hate in a person for him to kill. Last night was a stark reminder why we must stop the left. We must break up their power and free ourselves from their jurisdiction with states' rights. And we must develop a strong, God-loving conservative mainstream media that will introduce truth and reality to the rank-and-file Democrat voter.

Once we get our mainstream media and entertainment vehicles going, we must highlight in our media the way of life in conservative areas compared to those in the areas run by the left. We will highlight the fact that in conservative areas, people have more opportunities and a chance to succeed because of conservative principles and Judeo-Christian values. We will show in case after case that certain behaviors and values increase one's odds of success in life and that other behaviors that are promoted and approved of by the Democratic Party greatly increase the odds of being stuck in failure. We will show example after example in our entertainment vehicles, as well as real-life examples, that it is one's behavior and choices that have the biggest impact on a person's life and that it is one's behavior that dictates how the majority of others react to one. We will make it clear that it is not the color of your skin, your gender, your sexual preference, or whatever that the vast majority of conservatives object to. What we greatly object to is being forced to approve of and excuse behaviors in others that are harmful to themselves, to others, and society.

Then we need to put out warnings in our conservative mainstream media to all those working in police departments or in neighborhood watch programs that as far as some liberal Democrats are concerned, they are expected to show complete restraint even when having their heads pounded against a concrete sidewalk. If you defend yourself while being attacked, you will come under extensive criticism and scorn by those in the liberal community, those in the liberal media, and Democratic Party officials. You will be held personally responsible for the actions of every drugged-up twit that you have to deal with. In the minds of the Democrat officials and the liberal media, the police are completely responsible for anything and everything that can go wrong in dealing with their constituents in the communities that they control, even if their constituents are committing crimes, attacking you, spitting on you, cursing you, or whatever they do. It does not matter. You will be dragged into classes designed to teach you to be more sensitive to the feelings of malcontents and those committing crimes without any effort on the part of the Democrats in office to hold the criminals and malcontents accountable for their behavior. In other words, the Democrats and liberal media demand the police do more to make communities safer, but they then attack the police officers and take the side of the criminals and malcontents in every case, regardless of the facts if they can use that incident to advance the image that they, the Democratic Party, watch out for the minorities. And an image is all it will ever be because in reality the Democratic Party uses minorities as a stepping stone to their own power and wealth, and they have been doing so for generation after generation, always getting the minority vote on false promises and ginned-up hatred for the other side. The Democrats have no intentions of ever fixing the problems in communities that they create. They only intend to shift the blame to other communities and other political parties. So for all you who truly want to go into these troubled areas that are run by the Democrats and their policies and make things safer, *beware!* You will be put in a damned-if-you-do, damned-if-you-don't situation by the very people who claim to care the most—the Democratic Party.

We will also remind the masses that not too many years ago, the Democratic Party accused more affluent communities of not caring about poor black communities. They said those communities had rampant crime and that the people who lived in those communities were afraid to walk the streets. It was true. Where the Democrats ran the show in these poor communities, crime, gangs, drugs, and violence were rampant. So we as a nation promised and delivered more police forces to protect the citizens in those communities and crack down on the thug offenders destroying those areas. Fast-forward to today, where these same communities still led by the Democratic Party are now accusing the police of harassing and killing the people in those communities for no reason. Nothing is further from the truth. What is true is that the Democrats who run those areas are putting the police and all of us who believe in law and order in a no-win situation. When there is a high crime rate in these poor Democrat-run areas, the left blames the police and others that don't live in or have fled those communities for not doing enough to make those areas safe from crime. So when the police are called in and start cracking down on the troublemakers that commit all the crime, the Democrats and liberal media ignore the crimes that are committed, ignore the reality of the situations, and claim that the police are racist and are picking on minorities. The police officers' moves are scrutinized while the actions of the troublemakers are given a complete pass and they are made into victims. This, of course, has emboldened the criminal elements within these communities, and crime in these areas is as bad or worse than before. This situation will never change as long as these communities continue to believe in the lies of the left and continue to depend on the policies of the Democratic Party.

We conservatives need to be brutally honest with those communities that if they are going to continue to appease those behaviors and the people committing the crimes, then those communities will continue to suffer. Right now, any conservative saying that in the current liberal mainstream will get crucified, and the true problems will be covered up in favor of the false premise of racism as to the reason those communities are down. Once we can compete with the left in the mainstream media in strength and numbers, the left will lose their huge advantage they have in influencing the masses. When truth and reality can finally be told in the mainstream without being drowned out or ridiculed by the left, then the masses will start to see what we who listen to talk radio have known for decades.

Well, since I wrote the above over a year ago now, we have had more officers killed by this movement of hate that is a product of the leftist Democratic Party and their controlled mainstream media. This movement of hate is a glaring example of our irreconcilable differences with the left. The more we are being forced by the federal government to compromise and find common ground with these leftists, the further into the gutter we go. We must break away from the jurisdiction of the left and use states' rights to do it. Then we must accurately document areas run by God-loving conservatives in our mainstream and compare them with those run by liberal Democrats so the masses can see the stark differences.

Once we compete with the left's mainstream media, they will no longer be able to hide their failures and cover up our successes. The truth will win out, but only if we blast it from every media outlet at our disposal in every possible format so the masses can't miss it even if they try. We will explain why we honor the police and all those who work to protect us. We will also show what our protectors have had to endure from those on the left and that not all minorities hate the police. We will do this with public service announcements and talk show segments. Then we will reinforce those efforts with scenes in movies and shows. For instance, we could have a scene with an officer who just worked a traffic accident where a family of color was killed. The officer is emotionally shaken and grieving over the loss of life when he is approached by a man who taunts the officer and calls him a pig that does not care about people of color. The officer just keeps walking, but when he goes past a young girl of color, the officer hears her say, "Thank you for trying to help." The officer turns and looks at the girl, who then tells the officer that not everyone agrees with those who hate the police and calls them names. She says, "But we can't say anything or stick up for the police, because then others will make it bad for us." The officer smiles at the girl and says he understands as he walks by.

We must directly challenge the narrative of the left with a constant stream of scenes like the above, segments in entertainment talk shows, PSAs that promote the police and condemn the left, and positive posts about police in social media exposing negative posts by the left and their unfair treatment of those who work to protect us. I do see some conservative stuff trickling out into the mainstream, but we have got to open the floodgates. We must have a constant stream that flows out of our mainstream media that works in conjunction with talk radio and our conservative news sites that honor those who protect us, honor those with our values, and honor the American way of life that stands for freedom and opportunity for all people.

As incidents pop up and the left scrutinizes the actions of police officers to the nth degree in their media, we conservatives will scrutinize the perpetrators' actions with the same degree of scrutiny and report the findings in our mainstream. I predict that the vast majority of the time, you will find just cause for the officers' reactions to the situation because we will take into account that an officer never knows everything about a situation when answering a call, including the intent or capabilities of the people being encountered. An officer must attempt to prevent any and all situations from escalating dangerously while protecting lives and property and enforcing the law.

Then we will inform the masses in our mainstream that the Democratic Party and their liberal supporters want to put the added burden on our law enforcement officers of being responsible for the actions of an unruly, disrespectful, and at times even hostile public. In our mainstream media, we must inform the masses that this is just one of many irreconcilable differences we have with the left. We conservatives believe that each individual needs to be responsible for his or her own actions and suffer the consequences of those actions when warranted. Therefore, we must make it clear that those living in conservative areas are expected to be respectful and compliant when dealing with law enforcement or suffer the consequences of their actions. The reason for this is not so the officers can experience power trips but the recognition that officers are expected to maintain safety and order. So if a person is unruly, he or she must be dealt with swiftly in an attempt to maintain safety, enforce the law and keep any situation from escalating out of control which can lead to life or death situations. If anyone has a complaint with any officer on how he or she handled a particular situation, that person needs to know that he or she is free to file a complaint and is encouraged to do so in order for both sides to see whether the situation could be handled differently by either party. And both parties will, on those occasions, be reminded of what is expected of our law enforcement officers as well as what is expected of our citizens. This is how to have a safer community, and any community can adopt these methods or continue down the path of decay that is offered by the Democratic Party.

An Open Letter
to Democrats

Dear Democrats,

THE DEMOCRAT VOTERS OF today epitomize why big government and socialist-type policies do not work. You have hordes of rich liberal Democrats on your side that have net worths in the millions, and even billions, of dollars doing all the things the politicians and average Democrat voters claim to despise. Oh, some rich liberals give to charities and create foundations with their names on them, but so do rich conservatives that get chastised by the left. The rich liberal Democrats also buddy up to politicians, buy favors, spend money on mansions, fancy cars, designer clothes, and first-class lifestyles instead of living with modest means so they can give the rest to the poor.

The middle-class union types that overwhelmingly vote Democrat do so to protect their own benefits, even though not everyone gets those same benefits. Is that fair and equal? Why do they not agree to take less, if necessary, to ensure all get the same benefits regardless of the work put in? Is that not what Democrat politicians say—that people should support those who don't want to work? And as for the poor, not all, but far too many, are looking for ways to get handouts and are not even trying to support themselves.

All you Democrats need to stop blaming others, come together, and make your ideas work. But unless all you able-bodied Democrats agree to do equal amounts of work—because goods and services don't magically appear—consolidate all your money, and distribute it equally so everybody makes the same, then, and only then, does your socialist utopia have a chance to work.

So, dear liberal Democrats, make your ideas work with your fellow Democrats, and please let those of us that do not want to live in your big-government socialist world live in peace.

Sincerely yours,
Conservative America

A New Kind of Globalism

ETTING UP TO SPEED in the mainstream arena so the liberal media and entertainment industry loses its ability to have the amount of influence on the masses as it enjoys today is actually just the beginning of what we God-loving conservatives in our country need to do. We need to encourage our fellow conservatives across the pond and across our borders to also challenge, compete, and then defeat the mainstream media and entertainment industry in their countries as well. Then we must form an international bond of friendship and highlight their efforts to replace propaganda in their news in order to get the truth and reality out to their people. And just as important, we must highlight in our mainstream their efforts in getting the word out to their misguided masses on how conservatism, freedom for the people, and capitalism produce more opportunities for people to improve their lot in life when it is not reserved for just the chosen few.

We will show the misguided masses, in a steady stream of news and entertainment, that there are millions of people all around the world that have been negatively affected by the policies of liberals and ruling-class establishments. The mainstream masses will finally see there are millions around the world who are fed up with being ruled by the establishment types on either side of the aisle and forced to live with the aftermath of their policies. It will be the beginning of a different push for globalism. It will be a movement of globalism for God-loving conservatism that brings freedom and opportunity to the people all around the world, as well as truth and reality in the news, as opposed to left-wing propaganda and the establishment who downplay the antics of the left in order to push the compromise / common ground theme for their own gain.

Just as in our country, the mainstream media and entertainment industries of other countries are controlled by those who push government control over the people. Brexit proved that there is still hope for Europe. And I believe there is hope for all countries if we God-loving conservatives can stay the course, lead by our example, and avoid defeating ourselves in the process.

THE BEST OF THE BEST AND THE RULING-CLASS ESTABLISHMENT

ONE OF THE PITFALLS to avoid so we don't defeat ourselves is to never again allow a ruling-class establishment to pull the wool over our eyes. We conservatives must acknowledge the fact that the Democratic Party was right about something. They were spot on when they said that the Republican Party cares only about their rich cronies. We conservatives learned the hard way, watching events unfold from the times of the Reagan era to the present, that a sizable percentage of our Republican Party leadership was indeed looking out only for the elite and just presenting lip service to we the people. And regardless of what they say or do now, we conservatives must keep up our guard and shield our conservative areas from their jurisdiction as best we can by using state and county rights because the establishment types are only in it for the money and power they can secure for themselves. And when conservatism and power to the people win, the establishment types lose because it limits their power and access to what they believe is a never-ending money supply. It is also the reason why they would rather see a Democrat win than a conservative or anyone else who wants to drain their swamp.

Another pitfall to avoid is to allow the supposed best of the best to gain a near monopoly in the business world. This is a surefire way of keeping a ruling upper-class establishment forever entrenched in wealth and power over the masses. There are always going to be people who are blessed with certain attributes and will be able to run rings around most of us, and those people can usually rise to the top more easily than others. That is just a fact, but they should not be able to shut the door on the rest of us trying to make our way once they rise to the top, and far too many of them do. There are always going to be those who were born with advantages over others. That is just a fact, but they should not be able to use their advantages to shut the door on the rest of us trying to make our way, and far too many of them do. Now, don't get me wrong; I don't care, and I don't think anyone else should care, how successful a person or business gets or how much money a person or business has. That is not our business or the problem. The problems occur when people use their wealth and power to create obstacles for other people and their businesses in an effort to keep them down and eliminate competition so they can get more of the pie.

Now for those who think nothing needs to be done about those types of business practices because that is just business, well, the business and political upper-class establishment types are very grateful to you for thinking that way, because it helps them get to where they are and stay there. But the rest of us need to realize that if we don't put a stop to the obstructionist practices of some in the business world, then we will continue to be under the thumb of the establishment elite that cares only about maintaining their upper-class existence at the expense and oppression of others. Those in the business world that use their wealth and power to throw roadblocks in front of their competition in an effort to squash the chances of anyone else succeeding are the same types that buy government politicians for their own gain. Oh, we conservatives may win an election or two, but more often than not, the establishment will be pulling many more strings over us than they should. We must be able to spot and expose in our mainstream the politicians that sell out the American people and allow themselves to be bought in order to use their position to advance their own personal power and glory while they line their pockets with our tax dollars. And we must expose those in the business world who buy those politicians in order to get sweetheart deals for themselves and their businesses. Conservative talk radio, with Rush leading the charge, does an outstanding job of exposing these jackals. We just can't get enough on our side in the current RINO leadership to do anything about it, because they are a part of it.

Even us right-wingers must acknowledge the need for rules and regulations that will protect the average citizen and their businesses from the piranhas of the business world. Much more needs to be done in the area where big business throws roadblocks in the way of other businesses, especially smaller businesses and those just starting out. It is sad that provisions like these must be put into place, but it is just a sad fact of life that there are people among us that have no problem gumming up the works for the rest of us, in pursuit of their own personal gain and glory. Again, we should not care, nor is it our business, how successful someone is or how much advantage they may or may not have had. That is not the problem. The unscrupulous obstructionist practices some people and business groups use to get ahead and keep others down are the problem. Now, I am not talking about keeping any company from making the best product it can produce and competing in the marketplace. I am talking about things such as making it harder and creating obstacles for other businesses to get their products made and out into the market. And that is just one example. Unfortunately, there are many more that all need to be identified and dealt with.

All these unscrupulous ways used by some in business to get the edge over their competitors need to be exposed and done away with as much as possible. The goal here is not to control business but to open the floodgates of entrepreneurship and give all businesses a chance to sink or swim without the fear of being torpedoed by these unscrupulous business practices. This is how you look out for the little guy and gal—not the socialist Democrat way, but by giving all a chance and a shot at success and the opportunities to make their dreams a reality. This is also how you keep socialism at bay because more people will be in control of their own lives instead of feeling stuck in a job working for the man. So returning capitalism to the people and protecting our entrepreneurs from the unscrupulous business practices of others are the challenges and issues each state needs to be focusing on instead of being forced to deal with things like who can use which bathroom, which the feds decided to make an issue.

As we move forward, it will serve us well to remember that the best of the best are those among us who are at the top of their game and work to put out the best products or services that they can provide. And they should be encouraged to produce because many of them create good things. But as soon as they attempt to monopolize, buy favors from government, and block the advancement of others, then they cease being the best of the best because the best of the best want what is best not just for themselves but for others as well. And we should highlight those in business that are truly the best of the best positively in our mainstream media and hold them up as role models so more will aspire to be like them.

WE CAN'T RELY ON THE
FEDS TO FIX THEMSELVES

ANOTHER PITFALL TO AVOID is to make the mistake in allowing the federal government and all their agencies of bureaucrats to fix themselves and limit their own power. If we do that, it will never happen. Conservative states and "we the people" are going to have to lead the charge and demand an audit of the federal government each and every year. Then all federal tax dollars from conservative states should be sent to the state capitals first so that after the yearly federal audit, each state can decide what it will and will not pay for. Each state should be allowed to determine what it wants Washington to do for it and negotiate how much those services will cost, which will determine how much of its tax dollars go to Washington, how much stays with the state so it can handle its own needs, and how much goes back to the people. And our US senators and congressmen should spend the bulk of their time in their home states to determine these matters. With technology the way it is, our elected US representatives can now spend the bulk of their time in their home states and districts. They should go to the swamp of Washington, DC, only if absolutely necessary. Thanks to technology, our US representatives can vote and hold their meetings and hearings from their home states and district offices. It will be harder for them to sell out their constituents in favor of the Washington establishment if they are forced to stay in their own backyards.

If big federal projects need to be done, the voters can vote on a bond package that expires once the work is done. And as for the military, we conservatives need to realize that our military would run more efficiently and effectively if we got liberals and their money out of it. Those on the left can spend their money on "kumbaya" outreach programs and worthless treaties with other nations. Those on the right can restore the greatest military power on Earth.

There is no doubt an audit will show that the feds are not good stewards when it comes to handling money and should be put on a short leash. I predict that the rank-and-file Democrats would be just as appalled as conservatives if they saw how the federal government handles money, how it is spent, where some of it goes, and how much is wasted. The power is in the money. This is why an audit of the federal government needs to happen, and it needs to be an ongoing thing in order to truly drain the swamp because our federal government is so entrenched in corruption and cronyism that happened long before President Donald Trump.

Only the people and the states rising up in huge numbers can clip the wings of the feds and limit their role over the people. And when we have a mainstream media and entertainment industry that has the guts to tell the truth to the people and stand up to power instead of looking for ways to enrich themselves by jumping in bed with it, we will have a fighting chance for David to beat Goliath.

WE HAVE TO DO
WHATEVER IT TAKES

W E MUST NOT FAIL to do whatever it takes to keep ourselves separate from the left. Conservatives in each of the states need to focus on how we can preserve the Constitution and our freedoms by protecting ourselves from falling under the jurisdiction of liberal Democrats and those RINOs that want to whittle away at our freedoms with every common ground compromise. Hopefully defeating the liberal and establishment hold over the mainstream media and states' rights will be the answer. That way each area and its ideas can compete with each other and we will have an honest media in place to report the facts. But in addition to that, conservatives must be prepared for anything. And one of those things is the ability to move to our own currency if push comes to shove.

As we know all too well, the Democrats run up debt to gigantic proportions and take living beyond one's means to a whole new level. Therefore, I think it would be a good idea to slip into our mainstream programming reinforcing trickles pertaining to how easy it could be for the average person to deal with different currencies in this age of technology. People are already being conditioned away from actually handling money, so it is a perfect time to start conditioning people on using different currencies. And all we would need to do is show in our mainstream people buying things in different currencies with the slide of their card or the wave of their phone.

Hopefully, we conservatives would never have to move to our own currency. I would hope that just the threat and the reality that we could and would do it would be enough to rein in the spending habits of the left. And even if it didn't slow down the spending habits of the left, others might be less inclined to carry the debt of liberal areas if they thought there was a real possibility they could be left holding the bag. But our conservative leaders need to be prepared and have a plan in place if the day comes where we have to dump the dollar because the liberals have destroyed it. Now, when we talk about such things, the left will accuse us of being extreme and wanting to break up the union. That is when we must make it clear that conservatives do not want to break up the union. We conservatives just want to restore the power to the people and their states so right-minded people will have somewhere to go to get away from power-hungry know-it-all liberals and their RINO friends. Because we on the right have irreconcilable differences with progressive liberal Democrats and their ways of forcing their policies down the throats of the American people who do not want them, funneling money from conservative states to liberal coffers, spending money we do not have, printing money beyond our means to back it up, and raising the national debt without any regard to what these things do to the economy, the country, and future generations.

We need to make it abundantly clear to the Democratic Party and their voters that their goals and policies are in direct opposition to what millions of Americans want and believe in. But in addition to our policy differences, we conservatives have witnessed progressive politicians in power cover up blatant corruption and crimes on behalf of the members of the Democratic Party while ruthlessly going after anyone who disagrees with them by scrutinizing those people to the nth degree and holding them to standards that Mother Teresa would have found hard to live up to. So for this reason and all the other ways of the left—too many to mention because then this book would be longer than the Obamacare bill— is why we conservatives fight to preserve our Constitution and restore the power to the states and the people so we can be protected from those in the Democratic Party and their RINO friends.

COMPASSIONATE CONSERVATISM

W E HAVE ALREADY SEEN how RINOs want to show the world Republicans are compassionate; they do so by throwing our hard-earned tax dollars at liberal causes and calling themselves compassionate conservatives so the left will see that Republicans do care. This, of course, does not work. So the first thing we true conservatives need to do is drop the term "compassionate conservatism," because we God-loving conservatives have more compassion for people in the tips of our little fingers than the average liberal has in his or her whole body. But because of the constant barrage of liberal assaults in the media, we on the right find ourselves needing to prove to the masses that we care. Our efforts in the mainstream showing that enabling is not caring will go a long way in correcting the liberal narrative that conservatives don't care about their fellow man; but there is more we as conservatives should do—not to prove to liberals that we care, but to prevent more people from falling into the dependency traps set by the Democratic Party.

We conservatives need to recognize that not everybody responds well to tough love and that being bullied does not make everyone stronger. Tough love can be too tough for some people, and we should not just move on in a survival-of-the fittest mentality. And relentless bullying has destroyed childhoods, caused lifelong emotional scars, creates unnecessary distress in the workplace, and can lead some to violence and suicide.

As for tough love, conservatives need to showcase why we use tough love and how it has worked for so many. And for that reason, there should always be a place for tough love tactics. But we are all different, and different people respond to things differently. So we conservatives need to always promote various ways to help and motivate people to be self-reliant and not be too quick to expect that everyone will be able to pull himself or herself up by his or her bootstraps. If conservatives want to maintain solid majorities over the socialist Democrats in the long term and help more people in the process, we must be forever vigilant in finding and promoting more ways to help all those who want to be independent from government dependency succeed at becoming independent.

And as for bullying, conservative areas need to be a strong force against those who bully others and make their victims' lives miserable. And I am not talking about friends who harass each other, but those people need to make sure the targets of their antics are their buddies and not their victims. Because if it is determined their targets *are* victims, their punishment should be swift, and restraining orders should always be an option for the victim. Criminal charges could be brought up if the bullying behavior does not stop. We should never go down the path of criminalizing words, but the use of restraining orders provides another course of action to levy criminal charges on the bully for violating the restraining order if the bully does not stop his or her behavior toward the victim. It is without question that conservatives need to do a better job of protecting people who need protecting against bullies who get their jollies from tormenting others. And this is especially true when dealing with children still in grade school or those who are mentally challenged.

Now, unfortunately too many people have been taught by liberal Democrats in our schools and in the liberal media to actively seek out things to be offended about, and as a result, far too many innocent people have been falsely accused of bullying and harassment. Because of this, we need to help the coddled masses better determine whether they have just encountered someone that thinks and expresses himself or herself differently because that person lives outside the liberal groupthink bubble or if he or she has been truly bullied or harassed. In order to help these coddled masses, we should have training classes of our own to counter those sensitivity training classes the left forces many on our side to attend. And in our training classes, we should show true bullying, with videos depicting scenes such as a group of people picking on a teen wearing a "Make America Great Again" hat. The scene could show the group taking the teen's hat and threatening him with harm if he ever wore a hat like that again. Then the words "This is bullying" could scroll across the screen. Then show a scene where a group of four is walking down a sidewalk when a man driving his truck covered with American flags and pro-Trump bumper stickers taps his horn as he passes them by, causing the group of four to drop down to their knees and shudder in fear. Then words scroll across the screen: "This is not bullying."

Another scene we can show is a boss saying to one of his female coworkers in a private conversation that if she wants a promotion, she has to earn it in the bedroom, and he rubs her arm in a suggestive manner. Then a scroll across the screen informs the viewers that this is an example of sexual harassment because the boss is suggesting a work-related quid pro quo that is based not on job performance but on a sexual performance. Then a following scene shows the same two workers passing each other in the office hallway. As they pass, the man says to his female coworker, "Looking good." A scroll comes across the screen to inform the viewer that this is not sexual harassment. But the female worker has choices on how to handle the situation, such as taking the comment as a compliment, blowing off the incident as not important, or informing her boss that the comment bothered her. And, of course, she could take the matter up with human resources if such comments continued. But it is important to understand that comments such as those are usually not sexual harassment but are just the way some people give a compliment.

We can show all kinds of these types of contrasts, some funny and some serious, in a genuine effort to help the victims of liberalism that have been taught to be offended by anything that is not in line with their liberal way of thinking. We can end all our training videos by explaining to the coddled masses, in a genuine effort to help them so they don't go through life offended and in fear, that being overly sensitive is not healthy and that developing a thicker skin will serve them well. But more importantly, they should learn that people are different and come from all walks of life, so they express themselves differently and think differently. Unless you know what is in a person's heart, you should not be too quick to jump to conclusions and pass judgment on others based on the words they use to express themselves. And the overly sensitive liberal crowd needs to be told that they themselves have been offending people since the dawn of political correctness for their quick, judgmental responses to others.

FIGHTING FOR OUR OWN

ONSERVATIVES KNOW THAT WE are human and that humans make mistakes, misspeak, and so on. And most of those things should be quickly forgiven and moved on from. But that is not what happens, and that needs to stop. We cannot allow liberal forces to take out one of our own over gaffes or some other faux pas in our conservative mainstream media endeavors! When we do this, we only embolden our enemies and hurt ourselves. We who listen to talk radio know all this, but far too many that pretend to be on our side want to throw those who get caught up in the traps of the left overboard. These people are the RINO establishment types, and I said early on in this book that our mainstream media and entertainment industry must be filled with true conservatives that know the score and are up to speed on the shenanigans of the left because they listen to conservative talk radio. And this is one huge reason why: We have seen, all too often, these RINOs jumping into the spotlight with glee to side with the left and pressure our people to slink away in defeat over trumped-up, manufactured media hysteria. This is why our mainstream media and entertainment must be *owned* and controlled by true conservatives—so we will have a mainstream that works in conjunction with conservative talk radio and our conservative news sites to expose these hit pieces for what they are to the mainstream crowd.

We need to use all our media outlets to state the obvious (because liberals can't grasp the obvious on their own)—that conservatives have high standards but we are smart enough to know we are all imperfect humans who make mistakes from time to time. And we believe most mistakes should not cost a person his or her livelihood and destroy him or her. We conservatives must stand our ground against the liberal assaults and inform the people that those in the progressive press have lost all their credibility in telling anyone on the conservative side they should step down, regardless of the circumstances, because of the way they have ruthlessly gone after those on the right for every little misstep and blown things out of proportion. We will inform the masses that the liberal media routinely creates controversy and wall-to-wall hit pieces on those they oppose and then demanded firings, impeachments, and investigations on trumped-up charges with no evidence to back up their false narratives. We tell the mainstream crowd that the left-wing media sets people up with gotcha questions and stings to purposely trip up those they oppose so they can plaster that misstep all over their media outlets in an attempt to take that person out. And these liberal hacks in the media did all these things and more to undermine anyone who disagrees with their views while looking the other way on all the suspicious activity, antics, greed, crime, and corruption on the part of Democrats and their cronies.

Of course there are going to be times when conservatives step in it big time and need to go, or when some self-proclaimed right-winger commits an atrocity. These are just unfortunate facts, but we must not let the liberal media throw us all under the bus when these things happen. Instead we need to show the world how conservatives handle these cases as opposed to the left. When crimes and corruption occur and the perpetrator is obviously guilty, we on the right do not make excuses for the offender, do not make a hero out of the offender, do not make a victim out of the offender, do not riot over the arrest or death of the offender, or demand others understand why the offender did what he or she did and excuse the behavior. Then we point out that when the liberal media makes heroes out of criminals or makes excuses for them, it only emboldens others to do the same.

It is important to note that some on our side are stepping up their efforts to fight fire with fire and encourage others to call the advertisers of these liberal hacks and boycott their products or services in order to give the left a taste of their own medicine. We on the right need to make it abundantly clear to the left and the mainstream crowd that conservatives did not start these types of tactics. Because as sure as the world is round, the left will accuse the right of being bullies and play the victim card. We need to call out the ideologues and inform them that they should not dish out what they can't take and tell them that our efforts are just giving liberal hacks a taste of their own medicine. And while we are informing the ideologues that they should not dish out what they can't take, we should present a montage to the mainstream crowd in our entertainment projects of liberal talking heads and entertainers saying the most vile things about people on our side. And then, when our side fights back, we will show them crying like babies.

NEVER FORGET THE OBJECTIVES OF LIBERAL IDEOLOGUES

I N OUR MAINSTREAM, WE must address the sides, but we should not do so not when addressing the ideologues. We should drop the charade and call them out. We must guard against getting caught up in their sideshows and always remember that most of them really don't care about the things they claim to care about. If polls started to show immigrants that crossed over our borders wanted to vote out Democrats, the left would be rounding them up to kick them out while screaming for a wall. If polls started to show that the vast majority of blacks favored conservative Republicans and the vast majority of white men wanted socialism, you would see the biggest swap in the history of politics. And if polls started to show the transgender crowd overwhelmingly favoring conservative Republicans over the Democrats, the jackass party would not even fight for their rights to use a port-a-potty.

The liberal media's and Democratic Party's silence on the treatment of women and homosexuals in the Islamic world is proof, and just one example of many, that they do not care about the people they claim to be fighting for. And the fact that they look the other way on all the crimes, all the corruption, and a plethora of blatant improprieties committed by Democrats, all while going after non-RINO Republicans with a vengeance over anything and everything they can blow out of proportion in order to create a scandal, proves that they are not sincere but corrupt to the core. So whenever the liberal Democrats and their sycophants in the media go into a fabricated rage on one of their side issues, we should avoid getting caught up in their narrative. Instead we should rightly accuse the Democrats and liberal hacks in the media of going on fabricated outrages not to defend the offended or stand up to corruption but rather to silence those who oppose their views. And because of this, we on the right continue to make the case that those in the liberal media are not journalists but political hacks that have no credibility on any subject when it involves reporting on politics. And these liberals should be regarded as below tabloid standards when it comes to their reporting of the news. Then we will make it clear to the establishment that it is obvious to anyone with a brain that the liberal media covers the news the way they do because they want to get Democratic Party politicians elected so they can remain in the clique of power. And all the RINOs that buddy up to the liberal media obviously want the same thing! We conservatives know that most of these sideshow distractions, such as the Russians helping Trump to get elected, are just attempts to undermine a president or anyone else who wants to shift the power back to the people and drain the swamp of Washington, DC. And if every conservative would say that at every chance he or she got, instead of buying into the manufactured media hysteria designed to defeat freedom and elect control, then maybe we would make more headway. Because that is the real story on what is going on. And we need more than just talk radio and a few brave souls in our conservative media saying these things. We need to blanket the land with these messages.

The same thing can be said for political correctness. Most of us on the right know that the leftist hacks are not sincere with all their political correctness. It is nothing more than a tool used by the left to silence and suppress their opposition along their march to power. Yet too many on our side get caught up in it and attempt to appease the liberals, which is exactly how political correctness grew to be a problem for us and an advantage for liberals. It is funny, however, when liberal hacks get caught up in political correctness themselves and become a target because so many of the liberals' useful idiots embraced political correctness rhetoric as real. But all conservatives need to start seeing these pushers of political correctness as the political hacks they are and not as noble crusaders for the offended. When dealing with ideologues instead of getting caught up in their liberal narrative of political correctness and attempting to appease them, we should immediately call them out on playing the political correctness game. Then we should accuse them of passing judgment on people without knowing what is in a person's heart and assuming everybody can keep up with the all the words and expressions liberals find offensive these days.

Stop Interfering with Liberals Defeating Themselves

ANOTHER PITFALL TO AVOID is flexing our muscles over everyone else once our side has solid majorities at the ballot box. We can't just defeat the left in elections, rip the Band-Aid of dependency from their constituents, leave them pining for what might have been, and expect long-term success. So winning elections and forcing our will and ways on the masses because we know best is not the way to go. It is best to continue pushing for states' rights, preserving the Constitution, and putting pressure on the liberals to make their ideas work in their areas. Even liberal cities in red states should not be browbeaten into conservatism, self-reliance, and personal responsibility. Nor should red counties in blue states be subjected to liberal policies against their will. Instead, we should make it perfectly clear to the ideologues that conservatives do not want what liberal Democrats want and that it is time for Democrats to stop protesting, blaming others, bellyaching about how things are, and trying to force their ways on the rest of us. Instead liberal progressives need to embrace the freedom that this country gives us. Then they should pool their money and ideas together with other fellow Democrats all around the country and make their progressive plans work without dragging the rest of us into them and taking our dollars to support them. And when our mainstream media is pushing that it is okay to be different and exposing all the millionaires and billionaires on the liberal side saying one thing and doing another, it will be the perfect setup for liberals to defeat themselves. We on the right just need to make sure we put protections in place so we do not go down with them.

We must always keep in mind that many in the rank-and-file class that vote Democrat do not know how to handle freedom and independence, because they have fallen into the traps of dependency, but there is hope for those people. And I predict most will gravitate to the conservative side over time and give us a forever majority if we can keep the establishment types from fooling us again and regaining power. We must also realize that there are those who don't want to be free and independent in order to shield themselves from any responsibility. But luckily for us, there are forces that want to control people. So we conservatives need to link those two sides together and pressure those who push people into dependency to support their dependents. And those who want to be dependents need to go to the establishment Democrats and compromising RINOs for their wants and needs. And if either of those sides is not satisfied, then the dependent class and the ruling-class Democrats and RINOs need to compromise and find common ground with each other until they are one big happy family in their village. This, of course, will not fly with the Democrats and RINO elites, because our money is to pay for all the dependents they created. But we must not waver on this and demand that those who cause dependency pay for their dependents. And our mainstream media and entertainment for all the masses to see must keep their progressive feet to the fire, pushing them to support all their promises. And the Democrats and RINOs will have no choice but to either admit socialism has failed yet again or go broke trying to keep it propped up.

I am old enough to remember the big push for women to have babies out of wedlock, and all those who raised the red flags were crucified in the liberal media and entertainment industry. And all we hear today is how we have to help the single mother and all the kids growing up without fathers. And those people do need help because it is hard raising children as a single parent. It is also harder on the kids. But who pushed this lifestyle and actively encouraged women to have babies out of wedlock? The answer is the liberal Democrats. And we need to constantly throw that in their faces and rightly accuse them of doing this on purpose to make more people dependent on government. Because they did!

And as we all know, it is not just women that the liberal Democrats target to make into dependents. They also target immigrants. I remember back in the Clinton and then Bush days that those on the conservative side were pushing for immigrants coming into our country to learn English. And the liberal Democrats pushed back and argued that immigrants should not have to learn English. Instead, they said we Americans needed to start catering to those who speak different languages by putting out signs and messages in different languages so the immigrants wouldn't have to learn English and lose a part of their culture. Needless to say, my blood boiled when I started to hear liberal Democrats years later saying we need to do more to help the immigrants because many don't even know how to speak English.

Also, as conservatives know all too well, Democrats sought to make the majority of blacks look to the Democrats as their saviors, which is the reason many in the black community struggle to this day. It is not racism, but liberalism pushed by the Democratic Party, that keeps many blacks stuck in poverty. And we conservatives need to throw all these things in the faces of liberal ideologues and demand that if they are going to create a culture of dependency, then they need to support that dependency. And for those who seek that dependency, they need to look to the liberals in the Democratic Party to support them! Then, as the average nonelite Democrat voter begins to see what the Democratic Party and socialism truly have to offer, those who don't want to be kept can salvage their lives and free themselves from the shackles of dependency.

The war on drugs is another thing the liberals that support the Democratic Party snicker at and make fun of. They portray those who want to get tough on fighting drugs and keep drugs off our streets and away from our kids as fuddy-duddy types that want to ruin the fun of the cool people. And as usual, when people and communities struggle because of drugs, the liberal Democrats scream that we must help these poor souls and their communities. Well, those people and communities do need help. And those in Hollywood and other liberal hotbeds that not only promote the drug culture but also fight the efforts of conservatives to get drugs off our streets should pay for the consequences of drug use in America. We do need conservative-run programs to help those who want help, but wasting our tax dollars on liberal programs should never be an option.

Liberal Democrats also balked whenever conservatives wanted to help the people in other countries fight against poverty, terrorism, and tyranny in their areas. They called us warmongers and chastised us for wanting to be the world policemen. They also said we should not spend our money helping people of other nations when we have so many at home that need help. But they were just fine sending millions to the United Nations on a yearly basis to fix the problems. So after millions of dollars were wasted in the United Nations, making diplomats richer, the problems for the people have only gotten worse. And the Democratic Party's solution is to give more money to the United Nations and open our borders so people from other countries can flood in. This, of course, has made us all less safe and added more dependents to our society.

Unfortunately, there are many more of these types of examples and the liberals need to be called out on each and every one of them. So, hopefully more people will see that Democrats and their policies have caused more problems for people and their communities instead of fixing things. And while we are hoping their voters begin to see the light, we will relentlessly pressure the liberal ideologues in our mainstream to support their dependents and pay for all the consequences of their policies. But we on the right need to also showcase in our mainstream how conservatives want to help all those who want to break with liberal Democrats and learn a new way. We need to let the mainstream crowd know that there are alternatives to liberal ways and that conservatives want to help all those willing to help themselves. Our programs will be more like trampolines, as Senator Cruz has described them, to help people bounce back up instead of nets that trap people. And all taxpayer help should be documented in order to help distinguish between those who use these programs properly and get back on their feet and those who are seeking to milk the system and keep coming back to the trough. This will serve us well when we have to cut some people off. Because, no doubt the liberals will attempt to use them to show how mean the conservatives are. But we right-wingers will have documentation that we did try to help but some were cut off because we had reason to believe that those individuals were not trying to get back on their feet but were taking advantage of our system at the expense of other people. But if the liberals want to support that individual, they are free to do so. It will be interesting to see how liberal Democrats, with their phony bleeding hearts, react when they realize that their useful idiots are no longer their stepping stones to power but have become financial burdens around their necks.

It goes without saying that we conservatives need to continue to help those who cannot help themselves as a result of catastrophic illness or accidental injury, old age, or some other unfortunate circumstance and in need of care. And we do that because it is the right thing to do, and most of us on the right will have no problem with that. We just don't like it when we get taken advantage of by those able bodies milking the system. Of course, when those who seek to milk the system use their kids, those cases are especially challenging. But I believe more can be done to ensure that the money given goes to the care and feeding of the children and not for things like beer and cigarettes for their parents.

We need to send a clear message in our conservative areas to all able-bodied people who want to take advantage of our generosity and expect to get by mooching off of others that they need to go find a liberal Democrat to support them because catering to and enabling that kind of dependency brings down people and society. And if the liberal Democrats want to encourage that, then they can support it on their own dime! And if the RINOs and their constituents think we now must support those people because they have grown accustomed to their entitlements, they are free to donate their dollars to the cause.

We conservatives need to stand strong against the compromise / common ground narrative that keeps dragging us into the world of liberalism by pointing out the obvious—that we have irreconcilable differences in this country between the left and the right. We point out in the history of humankind that not once did everyone agree on everything; even among God-loving conservatives, we don't agree on everything. But that is the beauty of a limited government and freedom because we don't have to agree. We point out that we could peacefully coexist in this country if all sides would stop forcing their ways on everybody else. Sure, there would be some nationwide laws relating to things like not killing each other unless it is done in self-defense and stopping at red lights. But on things like health care, we conservatives need to make it clear that we do not care if liberal Democrats want to own and operate hospitals in their liberal areas and provide free health care to whomever they want. We can remind them that they don't need to send their money to the government and then fight for the government to do it. They can keep the bulk of their money and do it themselves in the private sector. We can also remind them that the government does not have a good track record of doing these things anyway. The veterans' hospitals during the Obama years is just one example. But just because conservatives don't want liberal ideas, that does not stop liberals from pooling their money and resources together and doing the things they want done, such as forming their own community insurance companies that cover whomever and whatever they want so people going to the liberal-owned hospitals will be insured. The liberal-owned insurance companies can even set up booths at the liberal-owned hospitals that will insure people on the spot when they come in sick or injured. But if the liberals insist on doing these things through the government, then they need to work them out in their blue states or counties because we conservatives do not want to be a part of it. We know that those programs, whether run privately or through government, will end up being financial disasters and the goods and services provided for the people will be subpar at best. But we conservatives would love for liberals to prove us wrong, because if liberals could make their ideas work, they would finally leave conservatives alone and stop trying to force us all into their policies. But that, my friends, is wishful thinking.

We also must address the problem of migrating liberals. If you live in a red state, you have probably witnessed liberal Democrats who have messed up their areas beginning to move into conservative areas to find work or escape the high taxes or high crime in their Democrat-run areas. This, of course, begins to bring down those conservative areas because the incoming Democrats bring with them their same liberal ways, values, and voting habits. So to help protect conservative areas from these migrating liberals, we need to encourage these Democrats to stay in their villages.

To do this, we on the right need to point out that conservatives can live anywhere without putting additional burdens on their communities because we don't rely on government to provide for our goods and services to the extent the liberal Democrats do. And because liberals want the government to handle things for them to the extent that they do, it will be more advantageous and cost effective for Democrats to stay in their cities, so as not to overburden your collective resources in having to implement liberal programs and services in every town in America. Then all red states and counties need to put protections in place for their conservative businesses that will be pressured by Democrats to accept the welfare cards, food stamp cards, health care cards, or whatever entitlement cards are given out by the jackass party. We need to inform the liberal Democrats that they will need to have enough funds in those accounts that the red-state businesses will get compensated the moment the transaction is made, or the card will be declined because liberal Democrats have bad credit. So it will be the responsibility of the liberal Democrats to either keep those accounts funded with their money or encourage all liberals who depend on government programs provided by Democrats to stay and do business in their Democrat blue counties.

We should also use our future mainstream media to shine a negative light on those who flee their liberal utopias in order to escape the aftermath of liberal policies and bring their progressive ways and voting habits to their new hometowns. This will, hopefully help these migrating liberals get a clue as to why they moved in the first place. But that is probably too much to ask of the average progressive liberal, so each red state and county needs to have plans in place to protect its nonliberal population from being responsible for all the wants and needs of these incoming Democrats. It may become necessary for states to keep the tax dollars of Republicans and Democrats completely separate. The Republicans would be in charge of Republican tax dollars, and the Democrats would be in charge of their tax dollars. It would be an interesting thing to try, but it will need to be done in ways that afford anonymity for the people in order to protect them from political persecution.

Finally, whenever the inevitable strikes and liberal socialism crashes, we conservatives need to be prepared with our response, and that response should be that those on the right are always willing to help and teach anyone the conservative principles and Judeo-Christian values that we believe keep us on course. But to expect us to throw money into the bottomless pit of liberal Democrat policies just to keep them running a while longer will only drag us all crashing down.

As We Challenge the Left, We Challenge Ourselves

THE CURRENT LIBERAL MAINSTREAM media and entertainment industry is designed to guide the people down a path to depend on government for their wants and needs. Their mainstream encourages the people to drink from the trough of government dependency and discourages people to go down the paths that lead to knowing God, Judeo-Christian values, conservative principles, capitalism, and our Constitution.

Our mainstream media and entertainment industry will encourage people to go down the paths and take the more in-depth second step that will lead them into churches that teach God's word instead of liberal hatred, and also into studying the Bible and learning about Judeo-Christian values. Our mainstream will also encourage people to follow the path from the first step of mainstream news and entertainment to the second, more involved, step of consuming the news and information that are available on our conservative talk radio programs and conservative news sites, where truth and reality about the events of the day live. And as these lost sheep begin to come down the paths toward our second steps, we had better be ready. So as we are challenging the left to make their ideas work, we need to also challenge ourselves.

There is no doubt in my mind that it was by the grace of God that the United States of America did not go over the edge into a government-controlled abyss on November 8, 2016. I believe we were given more time to save ourselves, future generations, and those who have lost their way because of liberal influences. And we must not waste the time we have been given. All God-loving conservatives need to recognize that this is our time and we must challenge ourselves to lead by example. And we need to readily admit that we are not perfect and we all make mistakes. But when we get off track, we must try not to make excuses and instead get back on the right path. Together we can be that shining city on the hill and be an example for the world to emulate. But of all the pitfalls to avoid, there is one above all others, and that is the mistake of trying to make it on our own without God—because without God, we will fail. All of us God-fearing, God-loving souls need to challenge ourselves to get right with God, study the Bible, and learn what is expected of us. We all need to pray to God for guidance and put the Lord in charge of our lives. And we must not let anyone separate us from God, as the liberals try to do by using the courts and misinterpreting the separation of church and state in order to use the state to banish God, because without God leading the way, we will fail ourselves and fail all the lost sheep who we worked so hard to reach with our mainstream media and entertainment industry.

Thank you for reading my book, and God bless America.

About the Author

Bass Johnson is a twenty-five-year-and-counting listener of the Rush Limbaugh Excellence in Broadcasting Network for Advanced Conservative Studies. She is also the author of two children's books, The Kids on Prosperity Lane and The Kids on Prosperity Lane Reach for the Stars, which are books for young readers filled with short stories that teach kids about personal responsibility, determination, persistence, believing in oneself amid negativity, decision-making, and setting goals—all traits that increase one's odds of achieving success and that counter the traits of failure taught by the liberals, who condition kids to be dependent on government, be a victim, and know the location to the nearest safe zone.

She started her latest book, The Missing Links to Making Conservative Principles and Judeo-Christian Values the Mainstream of America and Rescuing Our Country and Culture from the Grasp of Liberalism, prior to the election of 2016 and wrote most of it with a nervous feeling in the pit of her stomach at the real possibility of Hillary Clinton becoming the president of the United States. And she finished this book with the realization that the fight to save our country from the grasp of liberalism is far from over and that one of the biggest obstacles to beating back the advancement of liberalism is the left's hold over our current mainstream news and entertainment—an obstacle Bass Johnson has shown in this book how to overcome.